THE SOUL PURPOSE METHOD

DISCOVER YOUR UNIQUE CALLING,
REAWAKEN TO YOUR TRUE SELF,
AND CO-CREATE THE INSPIRED LIFE
YOU WERE MEANT TO LIVE

Published by Kynosura Publishing: www.kynosurapublishing.com
Services provided by Paper Raven Books

Printed in the United States of America

First Printing, 2019

Paperback ISBN= 978-1-7332946-0-7
Hardback ISBN= 978-1-7332946-1-4

PRAISE FOR

THE SOUL PURPOSE METHOD

"I am looking forward to reading and rereading my notes of the realizations that I came to about my purpose. The combination of information and transformation was magic—each process offered something to me. So, thank you for putting it into the universe and inviting us all in."

—Kelly Fredrickson, President, MullenLowe U.S.

"Wow—truly transformative. You have no idea what a gift it was to me. I've already had four conversations today at the office around my experience and my mission of reaching and inspiring those in the deepest need with the brand's purpose and magic. I've enlisted significant minds internally who are lit up and ready to take action to make it happen. I feel like I have woken up."

—Kim Culmone, Global Lead Product Design, Barbie, Mattel

"I had never known about the ego and the True Self. I had always thought all those negative thoughts and the 'I can't do that's' were actually me—not just my thinking. Seeing that, I can now choose to let those thoughts go and choose new thoughts that fuel my creativity and productivity."

—Mimi Lam, Hong Kong

"Living life in alignment with your soul is no easy task. First and foremost, you have to get in touch with what's authentic about you. Your true self. It can be very hard at times to distinguish between what is truly your Soul Purpose, and what you think or believe is your Soul Purpose based on your upbringing and the normal indoctrination that occurs in life. *The Soul Purpose Method* teaches you how to recognize the difference between what is authentically you and what may be your facade. Having gone through the process personally, guided by Kirk and Licia, I can honestly say that it's made a real difference to me and elevated the joy and sense of purpose I now experience in my life."

—David Paine, President and Co-Founder, 9/11 National Day of Service and Remembrance

"*The Soul Purpose Method* has been a life-changing awakening for me. It feels as if I've shed my adult skin and reconnected with my childlike self—that bright-eyed innocent boy who loves nothing more than to create, express, explore, love, and make others laugh. Throughout the event, there was a lot of new information and experiences that helped me get clarity and recalibrate my north star. For the first time, I can proudly and loudly say, 'I AM AN ARTIST!' and that being an artist is my gift to the world that can make positive change. Thank you."

—Chad Rea, Artist

"For about 15 years, I've wondered what I'd do if I didn't do my current job. Was there something I'd find more fulfilling? Something that would align with my personal beliefs? Something I could throw myself into? I thought about it. Talked to friends about it. And did yet more thinking. And got nowhere. In *The Soul Purpose Method*, I found answers. I had a massive injection of inspiration and got more ideas than 15 years of pondering."

—Simon White, Chief Strategy Officer, FCB West

"BIG BIG BIG thanks. I got immense value. I love the ego vs. Soul Purpose being distinguished throughout. I am amazed at how much the ego has been sabotaging things that light me up. The Los York label is an amazing laboratory and testing ground for challenging the ego vs. the authentic voice. I found that I just need to keep showing up for the original commitment and not let little 'concerns' stop me. The team is lit up by it, and I am lit up by it."

—Seth Epstein, Co-Founder, Los York

"*The Soul Purpose Method* provided the guided space I was seeking to dig deeper within myself and explore what really matters most—a sense of purpose from which I can live and operate both personally and professionally. As a brand and marketing consultant, I am now focused on illuminating the magic intersection of a company's real 'why' with its commercial goals to build culture, communication, and achievement through authentic human connection with a purpose. It's good for business (especially in today's world) and the soul."

—Helen McCabe-Young, Founder and Head of Strategy,
CMO Executive Services LLC

"*The Soul Purpose Method* has been such a powerful experience. It provided the unique opportunity to pause, open up, and envision new and exciting life and professional paths. I now view my business with much more of a service mentality, which has made my work more rewarding and meaningful. I highly recommend!"

—Jordan Olshansky, President and Director, True Stories

To my mom and dad, Virginia and George Rester, for your love, devotion, and unbridled enthusiasm for me and my work. And to all who have been and continue to be my spiritual teachers, guides, and mentors—David, Gina, Taira, J-R, Ron & Mary, Michael, and Martin. Thank you for illuminating my path of Soul Purpose.

—Licia

To my greatest teachers, in the order Spirit brought me to them:
To my mother and father, Dorothy and Louis.
To my wife, Patricia.
To my sons, McKinley and Kevin.
To the souls who showed me the way, Mary and Ron.

—Kirk

TABLE OF CONTENTS

A HEARTFELT WELCOME

Welcome.

Welcome to what may be one of the true "before and after" moments of your life.

Your "before" may have included feeling that a life of joy, purpose, and meaning was elusive—something that other, more fortunate or capable people enjoyed but felt beyond your reach. For instance, have you ever wondered: *What am I really here to do? How can I find my purpose? Do I even have one?*

Or, instead, have you had a sense of what you are called to do, but you second-guessed it, or yourself? *What if I'm wrong? What if I'm not good enough to achieve it?*

Or, have you felt you simply lacked the time, money, or opportunity in your busy life to pursue your dreams? Perhaps you have felt you hardly have the time to fulfill all your current obligations, to keep all the balls in the air, let alone chase a personal mission. Besides, what if you let down those people who depend on you?

And if you did dare to take the risk and go for your dreams, where would you even begin?

If any of this sounds familiar, if you have ever felt that yearning and the frustration of not knowing how or what to do, then know this:

That feeling is actually the first step of the journey.

That feeling is the fulcrum between "before" and "after."

And you are not alone in feeling it.

We know from our work that you are a part of a growing movement of individuals, groups, organizations, and businesses experiencing the same feelings and asking these same questions. Questions that are crucial in resolving the lack of meaning, joy, and fulfillment that are pervasive on this planet. Questions that may also play a crucial role in solving some of our planet's greatest challenges at a time when solutions are very much needed.

What's more, the very fact that you *are* here right now, with this book in your hands, signals you have already ventured beyond your "before" and are beginning your "after." The journey of living your unique purpose and experiencing the aliveness, inspiration, and fulfillment inherent in it is already in process.

We encourage you to take a moment, go inside, and reside in the possibility of the following truths:

A life of aliveness, purpose, and meaning is fully available to you.

You have already begun.

You have all that you need inside of you for the journey.

And you are supported by a Universe designed to help you succeed.

Welcome to your "after."

Welcome to your Soul Purpose.

INTRODUCTION

"Don't ask yourself what the world needs. Ask yourself what makes you come alive, and go do that, because what the world needs is more people who have come alive."

—HOWARD THURMAN

What if what Howard Thurman proclaims above is the actual grand design?

What if that experience of aliveness is how the Universe exclaims to you, "Yes! You found it!"

What if there was a guide that could support you in the process of discovering and connecting with that aliveness and inspiration? What if this guide could also show you how to design and live your life's most meaningful and true expression in the world?

Our intention is that *The Soul Purpose Method* serves as such a guidebook.

In our years of work with all manner of individuals, from CEOs, artists, and entrepreneurs, to mothers, fathers, retirees, and college graduates at the beginning of their life journeys, we have discovered there is indeed a reliable path to avoid living a default life—a life on autopilot where we find ourselves simply going through the motions and prioritizing others' requests and expectations over our own—a life in which we rarely feel vibrantly "alive," as Howard Thurman describes. We have learned there is a reliable path to the ultimate summit of living our Soul Purpose and to the meaningful impact that summit can bring to us and the world around us. While the journey may have a multitude of steps, our many years of being Sherpa to countless travelers on this quest have unveiled to us three main phases to a successful ascent:

Intention + Liberation + Co-creation ⇨ Soul Purpose

1. **Intention.** As we stand at the foot of the ascent and eye a summit perhaps still hidden by clouds and mist, we establish a clear intention to set foot on that new and elevated terrain of our Soul Purpose.

2. **Liberation.** As we climb up toward our intention, we find that the only way to attain that altitude is to lighten our load by releasing the old ideas, conditioning, and

self-limitations that kept us ballasted to the valley below.

3. **Co-creation.** As we near this summit, there is the great discovery that we need not do it alone—and have never done it alone. The ascent has been designed to be easier and grace-filled when in tandem with the Source of Creation that is all around us and can come to our aid in any form.

We call this three-phase approach the Soul Purpose Method.

We don't propose this is the only path—every summit has many ascents. We *do* propose that this path is available to you if you have yet to experience what you would classify as your true calling, if you doubt you can achieve your calling, or if you know your calling but have yet to risk making it a priority. You will see all these challenges surmounted in this book's recounting of the diverse experiences of our clients, students, and loved ones as they too travelled this path. (Some of their names have been replaced for privacy.) The teaching, stories, and activities that make up this book and the Soul Purpose Method can support you as they have supported them. The contents of this book can help you cut away the chaff, distractions, and noise in your life to unite you with what we will call life's true glory.

If you're hesitant, feeling for some reason you are the *one* exception, that the discovery of your Soul Purpose and a life of meaningful impact in the world are for other, "more deserving and capable" people, then we have a very important truth to share with you:

That is impossible because your Soul Purpose is already within you.

It is impossible to not have what you are born with. It is impossible to not be what you already are. The summit is not "out there" to be achieved. The summit is inside you to be discovered. And as this book will reveal, you already have all the equipment needed to get there.

What Do We Mean by Soul Purpose?

Before we take our first big step together, it is important to define what we mean by the two words that greeted you on the cover of this book:

Soul Purpose.

For us, Soul Purpose is a deep inner calling unique to each individual, as well as the path that supports the fulfillment of that calling. Our Soul Purpose (calling + path) gifts us with the opportunity to unite three of life's most precious and profound experiences—feeling vibrantly alive, learning and growing, and being of service by making a meaningful contribution in the world.

By the way, "making a meaningful contribution in the world" does not imply needing to make a global impact, though for some that may be the case. Any authentic, heartfelt act of service is destined to have a meaningful impact, but it may not be possible for us to immediately discern what that is. We may invent a device that creates clean drinking water for millions, or

8

we may encourage a child to design a science experiment and as a result of that simple, loving act, 30 years later that child develops a cure for a disease. Or that child develops the self-esteem to live a happy and contented life. All are of immeasurable impact.

While we often do not know how the impact of our Soul Purpose will manifest, it is our belief that each of us has an inner source that is aware of, and can aid our progress toward, a myriad of positive outcomes. For some people, that Source is called God, for others it is Spirit, the One, Creative Intelligence, Presence, the Creator, Energy, Divine Love, Wisdom, or Grace—and those names are just from the two of us writing this book! We will use a variety of names throughout *The Soul Purpose Method.* If we do not use the term that most resonates for you, please replace it with one that fits best.

What Is Required for the Journey?

In our work with ourselves and our clients, we have witnessed again and again that both inner and outer transformation are required to effectively navigate this path of Soul Purpose. But what does it take to transform?

Certainly, it takes more than mere understanding. If it didn't, then a manual on flying would be the only requirement for a pilot, and training videos on surgical procedures the only prerequisite for being a member of the operating team. The absurdity of these examples points to our innate awareness that the process of growth and transformation takes more than merely acquiring knowledge. It takes experience and practice.

Thus, the inner and outer transformations that make up the path of Soul Purpose require first learning new insights and setting a context that will form a roadmap for the journey.

Experiencing these insights for yourself as you explore your inner landscape and as you take steps to enhance your life will move you from theoretical understanding to personal, direct knowing.

Finally, what matters is practicing this approach so that you can reside more fully and consistently in *and as* your True Self and, from that Higher Consciousness, live a life that is an authentic expression and celebration of your Soul Purpose.

It is the connection with your True Self that provides clarity regarding your Soul Purpose and guidance about how to manifest your unique contribution in the world.

What follows are our two individual ascents to Soul Purpose through the process of Intention, Liberation, and Co-creation, how those journeys brought us together to do this work, to write this book, and together experience the pristine and rejuvenating air at the summit.

◆ ◆ ◆ ◆ ◆

Licia's Story

One of my earliest memories, around age four, is of imagining myself on stage in an amphitheater filled with thousands of people. I can't recall if this was a dream or just a flight of imagination, but it is one that has informed and guided my path. It was emblematic of a clear inner sense, which I had from a very young age, that I was here to serve many people.

As a child and teenager, I was drawn to performing both in theater and dance, thus fulfilling the vision of being on stage. This, in turn, evolved as my interest moved from performance to producing and directing, and I enjoyed many successful years in the entertainment industry. But eventually the ego gratification of the prestige and success I was enjoying began to lose its luster. I wanted more. My original attraction to entertainment was to utilize the powerful medium to serve, but the programs I was producing were serving the commercial interests of the sponsors rather than the audience. My dissatisfaction grew, and I began to look at my career as "my golden coffin."

That was until I had enough. I was especially stressed at work, dealing with tight deadlines and employee challenges. Earlier that week, I had been talking—more like complaining—to a close friend whom I considered one of the most conscious people I knew. I shared with him how afraid I was to take the risk of leaving my job. What if I leapt and wasn't caught? What if my calling to serve was a pipe dream? What if I was deluding myself? I wanted a sign from God or the Universe (whatever was the Highest Source) that I was on track.

My friend's response seemed radical. "Why not ask? Ask for a sign. But don't ask for a little sign. Ask for something so clear, so obvious that you can't possibly overlook or misunderstand it."

It was a wild idea, but I was at my wit's end. So I tried it.

Shortly after our talk, I asked the Universe: "Give me a sign if it is time for me to leave my job. But I don't want a whisper. I want something so clear that I can't possibly deny it."

Later that week, maybe only a couple days after my request to the Universe, I was having a particularly rough day at work. My growing dissatisfaction coupled with my increasing intolerance of the status quo pushed me over the edge. In a rare and unexpected moment, I simply left work, took the afternoon off—an act totally out of character for me—and went to the movies.

I drove across town back to my neighborhood theater, where a matinee of Enchanted April *was playing. (Note: If you haven't seen this movie, treat yourself.) The story depicted a woman who was living a default, dreary life and the risk she took by following her inner guidance. I won't spoil the ending, but the movie lived up to its title.*

I recall leaving the theater and simply sitting in my car drinking in the theme and magic of the story. Then, suddenly, inexplicably, I burst into tears.

There was a part of me observing this that said something to the effect of, "Oh, it's sad, Licia is crying."

But then another inner voice rose up, "She's not crying from sadness. She's crying from joy."

In that moment, I realized the second voice was right. My tears were ones of freedom. As I connected more with that truth, I felt joy and then an ecstasy that I had never experienced before. I began to laugh out loud through my tears. My physical sight even shifted, becoming sharper and clearer. I was finally free! I knew in that moment that I had to resign my studio position, and that I was experiencing the expansion and elation of having crossed over to a new era in my life.

And then the most extraordinary thing happened.

I heard a voice that was clearly distinct from my own inner voice—a deeper voice that I had never heard before. The voice said, "Is this sign clear enough for you?"

The tone of that voice was filled with loving and gentle amusement.

I was stunned. I knew in that moment that this was the voice from the Universe answering my request.

I drove home and shared my incredible experience with my boyfriend (now husband), David, who was understandably bewildered at his crying, laughing girlfriend.

Though this experience felt completely natural and real, I simultaneously recognized that it could be fleeting. I knew I had to mark this event so I wouldn't be able to relegate it to my overactive imagination in the morning. I asked David to help me.

He agreed and asked me what he could do. I replied quickly, explaining that I wanted him to cut my hair.

His jaw dropped in shock. At that time, my hair was quite long, close to my waist. "How much do you want cut off?" he gulped.

"I want you to cut it off, all the way to just below my ears," I said with complete certainty. I simply knew, whatever he did, it would be perfect.

To his credit, he obliged me.

The next morning, hair in a (very cute) bob, I put in my resignation.

That decision inspired me to form my own company and to shift my focus to the newly emerging "interactive edutainment" industry, which combined interactivity, entertainment, and education for children's products. In a matter of months, I began to fulfill my earlier desire to use entertainment to serve the audience, but it didn't stop there. My training and projects in the interactive space led to my involvement in the development of psychology software, which eventually led me to the University of Santa Monica, where I became a student of Spiritual Psychology and later a member of the faculty. Each of these major moves (and scores of choices in between) was predicated upon inner guidance, an inner sense that directed me to the next stepping-stone along my path of Soul Purpose.

What started by stumbling into a connection with my Higher Consciousness—that authentic and enduring part of me, which I call my True Self—has over time become a day-by-day practice of connection, attunement, and alignment—perhaps more subtle in the experience but just as miraculous and magnificent in its result.

Today, my Soul Purpose is supporting myself and others in awakening to the love, joy, freedom, and majesty of our essential nature and in living lives that reflect and celebrate this awareness. As a coach, educator, writer, and soul-centered facilitator, I've had the privilege of working with thousands of adult students, as well as private clients, groups, and professional organizations on their journeys of inner and outer transformation. We share our victories and setbacks, our laughter and tears, but mostly we share the beauty and sacredness of this journey home to who we truly are.

Kirk's Story

At the age of 18, while lying in a hospital bed, I watched a doctor I had never seen before enter my room followed by a number of interns and nurses, none of whom would make eye contact with me. The doctor proceeded to pull the curtain closed around my bed, as if the sterile green fabric would somehow stop the news he was about to tell me from being heard by the other patients just six feet away.

"Kirk," he said, checking my chart to make sure he was getting my name right, "I have some bad news. The mass we removed from your thigh was a very large synovial sarcoma."

"What does that mean? I don't know what that means." I said, now urgently looking at the eyes of the entourage for some hint about what he was telling me. Their inability to look into my eyes was telling me everything I was about to hear out loud.

"Well, it's a rare and aggressive kind of cancer." At this point, he looked around at his entourage, as if to signify to them that he was about to give "the speech." "You know, Kirk, most of the guys I treat here are jocks who I get to fix up and send back home better than new. I can't do that with you. This type of cancer is pretty relentless."

"So what does that mean exactly? Do I have to have that chemotherapy or radiation or something?" What I asked exactly in that moment remains fuzzy to me. All I knew was that he had said "cancer." He had most definitely said "cancer."

"No, I'm afraid chemotherapy and radiation aren't very effective for your kind of cancer. Kirk, people with this type of

cancer…well, like I said, it's pretty relentless. Particularly given the size of your tumor, it will most likely spread. People with this type of tumor can usually expect to survive another 18 to 36 months."

This was to become the "before and after" moment of my life.

What happened from that point was a many-year odyssey of radical treatment and surgeries. In the midst of it, I had a profound awakening to the miracle of my life. Cancer was both one of the greatest struggles of my life and also the start of a great awakening. Mortality shaking me awake from sleep at the age of 18 as opposed to 85, just moments before death, is a blessing that has driven my life. My tumor did spread to my lungs, and at the seemingly darkest time I remember saying to my parents: "I'd rather have had these couple of years awake than to have spent the next 60 asleep."

And I meant it. I began to live lucidly—not from the awareness that my cancer was terminal, but that life is. People with terminal cancer aren't different because they have a terminal condition—we all have a terminal condition. It's called life. They are different because they have simply become aware of it. Whether it was cancer in two years, a heart attack in thirty, or a stroke in sixty—this had become inconsequential to me. In a blink, or two blinks, or three blinks, my life would someday, relatively soon, come to an end.

I knew, not as information, but as a deep irreversible knowing, we are all in the process of dying.

Seeing that so clearly freed me. It freed me from the worry and fear around the little things that I had deluded myself into believing were giant things. I began to experience my Soul—this deeper, more real part of me—not as a concept but as a living reality. I remember being in a car heading home from Memorial Sloan Kettering Cancer Center in New York City with my father driving about a year after my initial diagnosis. We had just gotten the news that the original tumor had metastasized to my left lung. The fate I'd eluded now felt sealed.

We stopped at a red light on York Avenue. In somewhat of a daze, I was brought back to reality by a horn blasting and not ceasing. I looked at the car next to me. A man was leaning on his horn, the veins in his neck bulging, as he screamed at the red light as if it were killing his children because it was not turning green fast enough. I remember thinking: "Wow. That is just not a real problem. I will never be like that guy."

Soon, monthly scans became quarterly scans, became yearly scans, became biannual scans. I reached the five-year mark. I reached the ten-year mark. I reached the mark where your surgeon tells you there is a greater chance of getting a new cancer from all the radiation you've had than your original cancer returning. Without doctors being able to point to any particular thing, and having paid the relatively small price of losing most of my thigh and half of my lung, I made it through metastatic synovial sarcoma.

With survival becoming more and more real, I threw myself into college and then early years of work in New York City in the advertising business as an art director. Given my experience with cancer and a peek at the finiteness of life, I was driven by a desire to fully seize every opportunity with great engagement. At the ripe age 41, I had become the President and Chief Creative Officer of a large ad agency in San Francisco. I had also met the love of my life while in New York, gotten married at the boathouse in Central Park, and been blessed with two bright and beautiful sons, one ours biologically and one a blessing adopted from China. I had seemingly "made it" on all fronts.

But that was an illusion. One day, driving on the Embarcadero, I witnessed another man leaning on a horn and screaming at a red light that wasn't turning green fast enough. In one of the most dismaying moments of my life, I realized that man was me. I'd become disconnected from my greatest blessing. I was given the single greatest gift in life—the awareness to live awake to the blessing of this human experience—yet I had betrayed that gift by falling asleep again, becoming unconscious and treating life like it was a commonplace occurrence that could be wasted by yelling at red lights.

Seeing that I had become that man I'd sworn I would never become functioned like spiritual sniffing salts. In a matter of weeks, I made a series of abrupt changes. They started with the simple, personal vow to be awake and learn the tools I needed to stay awake.

I resigned from my corporate job, and soon I found myself in graduate school at the University of Santa Monica, working toward a master's degree in Spiritual Psychology. I learned how to distinguish between the voice of my ego and the voice of my Soul. One-by-one, I began dismantling the judgments my ego had placed between me and the reality of who I am. I found myself letting go of the limiting beliefs that told me my profession had to be different than what I did in service in the world, that what brought me alive had to be different than what I did to stay alive. I opened to my Soul Purpose as my means of sustaining and even thriving in this world.

My life became a process of Co-creation toward my Soul Purpose as opposed to a solo creation toward my ego's preference.

Twelve years later, I am still using those tools in my vow to honor the gift of my life by doing my best to stay awake. I say "doing my best" because what I've learned is that it's natural to drift off to sleep at times and that those moments are some of our best teachers for staying awake. Today, I am no longer the president of a 300-person advertising agency. Today, I am the co-founder of a 30-person heart-led company that creates positive impact at scale both through large cultural initiatives shared by businesspeople, philanthropists, government leaders, artists, and citizens, and through coaching high-impact leaders to follow their Soul Purpose.

My blessings sprung from the moment the doctor walked into my hospital room and told me I had a terminal condition. He was right. I do have a terminal condition. It's called my life.

While my life is inevitably terminal, if I am in my Soul Purpose, every single moment has the potential to be exquisitely beautiful, profoundly heart-opening, inconceivably creative, and infinitely loving. The blessing of being awake to having a terminal condition is that it forces me to ask the two questions that can unlock a lifetime full of all those qualities:

What will I do with the time I have left?

Am I willing to start right now?

That you are reading these words means you have already answered the second question. If you keep reading, you will inevitably answer the first.

◆ ◆ ◆ ◆ ◆

Licia recounts the magical moment that inspired their partnership:

Kirk and I both admired and respected each other, but we had no intention of partnering with one another until one fateful day when Kirk asked me to lunch. Kirk's coaching practice of helping business leaders find inner purpose was expanding, and he was considering designing and facilitating a workshop to serve the growing numbers of people interested in exploring their purpose. Knowing my background in workshop and curriculum design and my faculty role at the University of Santa Monica, Kirk asked if he could have my opinion about the best way to do it.

When I heard from Kirk, I was delighted to have the opportunity to support him. The experience was one of openhearted service, completely absent of any sense of obligation or thoughts of professional benefit. It simply felt like a fun thing to do. Looking back, this was my first spiritual breadcrumb, leading to a whole new chapter of my life.

When Kirk shared his project, I immediately fell in love with it and offered ideas about how he could design his workshop. The creative energy and enthusiasm were palpable until at one point Kirk stopped and declared, "I just got an idea! What if we did this workshop together?"

It was clear the idea was inspired. We both felt the electricity in that moment. And as the process unfolded, we experienced a grace and ease uncommon in the development and production of these types of offerings. We attribute this grace to us both letting the Spirit and the Universe in—allowing the best possibilities to unfold. This continued through the workshop itself and appears even now in the many stories we receive from participants as well as in our current work together, which includes this book.

We have spoken about the journey to Soul Purpose as an ascent to what can be an elusive summit.

Out in the physical world, on those treks to the highest, most elusive peaks, you will encounter what are called cairns—vertical piles of rocks to let you know you are on the right path. As you read *The Soul Purpose Method* and participate in its activities, you will experience moments that feel like a sudden remembrance—"aha" moments where you will say, "Of course! I knew that was somewhere inside me." Think of those moments as cairns set by your own Soul, letting you know that you are indeed on the right path.

Connecting to your Soul Purpose and the meaningful contribution you were meant to share with the world is just steps away.

—Kirk Souder and Licia Rester
Los Angeles, January 2019

INTENTION

SETTING YOUR SIGHTS FOR THE JOURNEY
AND CONNECTING WITH THE FOUNTAINHEAD
FROM WHICH CREATION SPRINGS

CHAPTER 1

ALIGNING INTENTION AND ACTION

"The qualities of creativity and genius are within you, awaiting your decision to match up with the power of intention."

—WAYNE DYER

I n the introduction, we shared an overview of the Soul Purpose Method—a road-tested approach that contains the key concepts, context, and practices for the Soul Purpose journey.

Now it is time to venture into the first of this three-phase method.

We start where everything in creation starts.

Intention.

Everything that comes into reality begins with an intention, from the creation of the Universe to the creation of a new business plan. Before there is action and before there is change, there is an intention. The creation of a life experienced in our Soul Purpose is no exception. It starts with a clear and well-defined statement of intention describing what our Soul Purpose looks and feels like to us.

As seminal as intention is, if it is not supported by actions and choices that are aligned with it, it is an exquisitely adorned golden carriage with horses pulling in conflicting directions. In other words, it is beautiful, but it goes nowhere.

Let's bring this into the real world. We wake up one morning and realize it is time for a change. We see time pass, seasons change yet again, another day emerges much like the one yesterday and the one before that. We feel a dissatisfaction growing inside us. We catch ourselves thinking more and more often: *There has to be more to my life than this.* This discontent increases until we make that powerful and life-altering choice for ourselves to begin the adventure and process of extricating ourselves from our default life and excitedly move toward our Soul Purpose.

New Beginnings

Typically, the first thing we do is set a singular and powerful intention (more on this later in the chapter) for the new experience we seek. We are clear in our desire to have a life and vocation of meaning, purpose, and aliveness. We become invigorated and energized, launching out into the world armed with our intention and confident that we will now have a front-row seat to the emergence and realization of our Soul Purpose.

The Universe receives our intention and provides us with opportunities we can utilize to live more fully in our Soul Purpose. Yet, as these situations get presented to us, our actions and behaviors still align with our default life as opposed to generating the new one we have set an intention to move toward. Instead of responding to the usual situations differently so that we stay in alignment with our intention, we keep making the same default choices. Instead of responding to new opportunities with choices that bring us to someplace new, we make choices that bring us back to where we were. And we wonder, "Why is my intention and Soul Purpose not unfolding in my life?"

Imagine you decide one day you have outgrown your current house and you want to rebuild and create a new one that better reflects who you are inside. You have a broad vision of the kind of house you would love to live in, and you hire an architect to bring that vision to life. You describe your vision to the architect, she listens intently, and you both excitedly give a thumbs up on a blueprint for your new and spectacular home.

Then comes the process of building it. Just when the old walls are about to be torn down, you say to the architect, "Um, maybe not *those* walls, I'm kind of attached to those." And then as new structures begin to be constructed, you say, "I know we spoke about wood there, but can we instead use the brick I had before—I'm very comfortable with that brick." And then when the windows are just about to be installed, you say, "Yes, I know we agreed on the floor-to-ceiling for the windows, but now I am preferring something smaller, something a little closer to what was there before."

The day comes for the big unveiling, and when you arrive you are dismayed to see that what is standing there is not what your vision or intention was at all. It is actually the same house you have been living in all along. You ask the architect, "What happened? Why is this my old house and not my new house?" The architect replies, "I don't understand. I know it's not what the blueprint was, but it's what you chose each step of the way—the same walls, the same floors, the same windows, the same roof. You may have envisioned something different, but when it came to making it real, you built it as you built the old house, and so that is the house you still have."

Conflicting Intentions: The Interplay of Intentions and Old Patterns

What this story illustrates is the powerful interplay between intention and old patterns. The way we act on our intentions can move us forward or hold us back from realizing and living our Soul Purpose.

Let's imagine the architect and the blueprint as the intention for our new life, and the building of the house as the actions and choices we make in response to our intention. We see that we can have the clearest and most powerful intention in the world, but if we aren't prepared to take new actions and make new choices, then it will be difficult, if not impossible, for our new life to emerge.

If we have created walls but are unwilling to take them down, those walls will keep us confined. If there are new experiences we want to have (i.e., the wood), but we keep choosing the old experience (brick), then that is the experience we will continue to have. If we want greater awareness and exposure to a new world, yet we keep choosing smaller windows for safety and protection, then our access will remain limited.

A common example of this dynamic can be found in Licia's personal story. She was dissatisfied with her job at the entertainment company. She yearned to use her talents and skills to make a more meaningful contribution, and she was clear that this new level of contribution required a move to new work opportunities. Yet, for years, she remained in her job. Not surprisingly, she experienced more of what she did not want.

What we are experiencing is the result of *conflicting intentions*. That is, we say we want one thing, but our actions communicate an intention that is at odds with what we say we want. This is one of the most common speed bumps to the realization of our Soul Purpose.

It is when our intentions and actions align that the power to manifest our dreams and Soul Purpose exponentially scales. If at every step of the way we choose and act in the direction of our intention even when it might push us past our zone of comfort and familiarity, we will find ourselves living our Soul Purpose. We will find ourselves living in a new house that inspires us and brings us alive in ways we had not even imagined. Our house will be a beacon for others who also yearn for something new. Our lives demonstrate the power of aligning intention and action, which can inspire others to do the same.

Setting Clear, Positive Intentions

How do we begin to more effectively utilize intentions in support of our Soul Purpose?

The first step is to create a clear, positive intention. In the years of work with ourselves and others, we have learned that setting clear and inspiring intentions is one of the most powerful actions we can take to ensure we are on course.

All journeys start with intention. Consider any trip you have taken. You first had to clarify where you wanted to go in order to buy the plane ticket, pack the right clothes, or properly plan your itinerary.

Even if the trip was a more spontaneous adventure of exploration and discovery, that approach *was* the intention.

The good news is you are already experienced at setting intentions. The opportunity you're being offered here is to become more conscious and conscientious in setting intentions. The clarity you gain from the process will support you to more effectively manifest your vision.

An intention functions as a conscious focus for you, as well as a clear request to the Source of creation. An intention can also provide an opening to greater inspiration, wisdom, clarity, and guidance. For example, as co-authors of this book and co-facilitators of Soul Purpose products and workshops, we set intentions each time we work together. These intentions support us in aligning with and attuning to our True Selves as conduits for Universal Creativity. We also set intentions every morning and throughout the day as part of our daily spiritual practices.

In the practice section below, you will have an opportunity to learn a process for setting clear, positive intentions to use both in daily life and as your Northstar Intention for your Soul Purpose. You will be utilizing this process of intention setting in a variety of ways.

However, as our earlier example of building a house demonstrated, it is not enough to simply create an intention. It is also important to act in alignment with that intention. As you'll see in the story that follows of one real-world architect, intention coupled with aligned action can powerfully support you in manifesting your Soul Purpose.

A Real-World Story: From Swamp Rat to Magic Kingdom Mouse

Licia's father, George, has provided her with one of the most enduring lessons of the power of intention coupled with action. The story he shared of committing to his dreams continues to be a source of inspiration for her today.

As a child growing up in the bayous of Louisiana, George lacked the amenities and privileges most of us take for granted. His family scratched out a meager living as subsistence farmers and loggers. After his father left unexpectedly, George was sent to an orphanage because his mother simply could not afford the cost of caring for him. Eventually, he was reunited with his mother, who was waitressing in New Orleans as a way to support her son. In the big city, George was introduced to a whole new environment and with it a growing desire to enjoy a better life for himself and his family.

Without knowing it, he had set his first intention. Following that, a simple act of kindness changed the trajectory of his life.

One afternoon, he noticed one of his high school teachers struggling with a large pile of textbooks. Rather than continuing on his way, he chose to cross the street to help her with her books. The two fell into friendly conversation. His yearning to improve his life prompted him to ask the history teacher if she knew of any groups of people who had striven to improve themselves. (In our current culture, self-improvement is second nature, but to a boy whose entire family lived and died in the swamp, it was a radical notion.)

The teacher shared about the men and women during the Renaissance period and encouraged him to learn more. He had never heard of the Renaissance and repeated the strange word to himself again and again as he hurried to the library. In his studies of the period, he came across the life and work of Leonardo da Vinci. Inspired by Leonardo's legendary accomplishments in art, invention, and architecture, George vowed to emulate this great master.

His new intention was clear, and he dedicated himself to what he called "the pursuit of excellence." In short order, his low grades rose. Aligned with his intention, he taught himself art and became accomplished in both sketching and painting. As Leonardo had, George began to observe nature and consider innovative ways of solving daily problems. This new approach to problem-solving was put to the test as he tackled his biggest goal—to become an architect like Leonardo.

The challenge was that he had little formal education and none in architecture. He was also reticent to earn a college degree. By this time, he was married with his first child, working and struggling to make ends meet. Once again, he looked to Leonardo. If his mentor was self-taught, so would he.

He bought a large tome, considered at the time to provide the essential information in the field. Over 1000 pages, this volume on architecture would provide the foundation for his personal course of study. The next problem was that his childhood years in and out of foster care had left gaps in his grade-school education. With his lack of reading skills, how would he ever get through the text?

Though he struggled with reading, his wife, Virginia, did not. Encouraged by her and recognizing the challenge as an opportunity to test his commitment, he bought a tape recorder rather than giving up. With a baby on her hip, Virginia read every one of the 1000 pages of text into the recorder during the day. When he got home at night, George would listen to her recordings.

They worked together like this for over a year. Then, it was time for George to take the architectural board exams. He passed on the first try.

But his victory was short lived. Noticing he had "forgotten" to include in his materials the name of the university where he had studied, the board examiners quickly discovered that he had not earned a college degree. They assumed the only way he could have passed the boards was to cheat. They held his exam status until he could prove himself by passing a second, oral examination. Sticking to his intention, George stood in front of a committee convened to test the veracity of his outrageous claims.

This time when he passed, it stuck.

As an architect, George yearned to combine his artistry with innovative design and architecture, like his mentor Leonardo did. He had a new aspiration and intention: "To create beautiful places where people want to be." Though he did not know it at the time, this would become the intention behind his Soul Purpose.

Once again, his clear intention coupled with his willingness to put in the effort paid off. His elegant and artful designs at the 1964 New York World's Fair were noticed by the innovative entrepreneur Walt Disney, who had his own intention of creating the "happiest place on earth."

Walt invited George to tour WED Enterprises, the Disney headquarters for the architectural group and theme park design in Glendale, California. George recalled that he felt as if he were dreaming. He said, "This one place housed the greatest gathering of artists, designers, and innovators that the world had ever seen. I would have worked there for free if I could have afforded to."

George accepted Walt's invitation to join his team of Imagineers. Projects for Disneyland, such as the New Orleans Square, led to the design of attractions at Disney World. His natural artistry, innovative design, and architectural expertise eventually led to him accepting the position of Chief Architect for WED Enterprises, with the design of EPCOT as his flagship project.

Decades later at George's retirement in 1987, the President of Walt Disney Imagineering wrote him a personal letter. In it, he shared that George was "an inspired Renaissance man."

This letter along with his oil paintings, charcoal sketches, and photos of EPCOT hang on the walls of his home to this day—reminders of the magic that comes through clear intention and devoted action.

Soul Purpose Practice

The practice of intention setting can be used in any area of your life. It is a powerful way to give yourself direction and make a clear request to Spirit.

Creating Intention and Actions in Service to Your Soul Purpose

This activity will support you in clarifying your focus, calling forward your energy in service to your Soul Purpose, and acting in alignment with your intention. Setting your intention can also provide you with the opportunity to gain maximum results from this book. (Note: If you are clear on your purpose, you can use this first activity to set an intention to deepen your understanding of your Soul Purpose and to create actions to continue supporting its unfoldment.)

We recommend you select a journal (or other favorite writing method) prior to engaging in this activity and dedicate it to your journey of Soul Purpose.

Take a few minutes to consider the following questions and write your responses in your journal.

1. If this book was wildly successful for you, what benefit(s) would you receive? In other words, how would your inner and outer lives be different?

2. How important is this level of transformation for you? How powerful is your calling to connect with your True Self? How strong is your desire to discover and live your Soul Purpose? How will this serve you and others?

3. Given your responses to the questions above, create an intention for clarifying your Soul Purpose. As you develop your intention, infuse it with your enthusiasm. Below are examples of some initial intentions:

   • My intention is to be open to new possibilities, inspiration, and guidance for my highest good.

   • My intention is to joyfully open to receiving clarity on my Soul's calling.

   • Given my skills, gifts, and interests, my intention is to attune to Spirit's Guidance regarding my highest good.

   • My intention is to easefully connect with my True Self and clarify my unique contribution to the world.

   • My intention is to honor myself and my true calling by fully engaging with this book and its activities.

- My intention is to joyfully open myself up to my journey of Soul Purpose and the revelation, growth, and inspiration that are available to me.

4. Once you have clarified your intention, the next important step is to consider and commit to actions that will support it. Consider one to three actions that would support the fulfillment of this intention. For example, an action may be to read one chapter of this book and complete the activities each week. Another action might be to state your intention twice a day, in the morning and the evening. A third might be to enlist a Soul Purpose partner or reading group for mutual support in this journey of discovering and living your Soul Purpose. Keep in mind you are not yet committing to any of these actions, so give yourself the freedom to write down any and all actions, however outrageous, that would support you in clarifying and co-creating your Soul Purpose. Write down the actions you have identified.

5. Review your possible actions in light of your intention. From the higher energy and enthusiasm of your intention, consider your list of actions. Do any of them jump out as ones that would be particularly effective? Put a star next to those.

6. Take one of the actions and respond to the following questions in your journal:

   a. What was your experience in taking the action?

    b. What did you learn?

    c. How did you feel?

7. Take a moment to acknowledge your willingness to engage in this process in service to living a life of joy, meaning, and fulfillment!

CHAPTER 2

ELEVATING FROM EGO TO TRUE SELF

"Have the courage to follow your heart and intuition.
They somehow already know what you truly want to become.
Everything else is secondary."

—STEVE JOBS

I t is not possible to connect with one's Soul Purpose without first connecting with one's Soul.

You may have a different word for "Soul," and that's totally fine. It may be Essence, Energy, Higher Consciousness, or the term we use, True Self.

This True Self, with a capital *S*, is different from the transient, small self (little *s*) that takes form during our human experience, which we call the ego or the personality. Being able to distinguish between the two becomes vitally important on the journey of Soul Purpose, as the True Self resides in a realm of infinite possibility while the other self exists in five-senses reality, which is characterized by physical and mental limitations.

You can imagine that the course the True Self would set in the journey of Soul Purpose would be vastly different than the one set by the constraints, fears, and risk-averse conditioning of the ego. That is why in this first phase of Intention, it is important to become more aware of these two different aspects of consciousness and how they function. With this understanding, you can more readily connect with your True Self and use its love, wisdom, creativity, expansiveness, and inspiration to set a Soul Purpose intention that functions as a true north star for your path. In fact, we call this type of Soul Purpose intention, a "Northstar Intention," for just that reason.

What follows is a dream that Kirk had several years ago when his own journey to Soul Purpose began in earnest. We include it here because it is a dramatic illustration of the difference in experience when one leaves the limitation of the ego to see life through the eyes of the True Self.

◆ ◆ ◆ ◆ ◆

Kirk's Dream

It began with me as a prospector, knee-deep in a cool stream with a miner's pan held firmly in both hands.

In a search for gold, I am dragging a pan through silt at the bottom of a stream then lifting it up through the water to wash away the brownish sludge in the hopes of spotting golden flecks and nuggets underneath. As I dredge the bottom of the stream, I am sure I am seeing quick flashes and sparkles of gold, and excitedly lift the pan up with high expectations. But upon diligent exploration, there is nothing there. Nothing.

My dredging becomes more frantic. Again and again I drag the pan with increasing force and desperation, and again and again, there is no gold there.

Finally, in exhaustion, I stop. I fall to my knees in the stream and let go of the pan, which sways its way into the silt and disappears.

Slowly, the water that had been made violently turbulent by my incessant clawing, begins to calm. And as it does, something odd begins to happen. In the slowing undulations of the water, I am again seeing more and more flashes of gold, sometimes even blinding me with their brilliance, causing me to close my eyes and open them only to a squint. With no pan, I can't do anything except kneel and witness the spectacle of it. Soon, the water has become absolutely still, but I can barely look at it as the golden luminescence feels too bright for me to bear. Gradually, my eyes adjust. I can focus on what is before me. When I begin to recognize it, I am at first shaken with fear. There, in the water in front of me, is the golden figure of a being—golden light beaming from every square inch of its body—its hands, its hair, its eyes. I am about to stand and run, when something causes me to stay. There is something familiar here. Our eyes meet, and I realize I know those eyes. I know the hat this being is wearing. I know the shirt this being has on. They are my hat, my shirt, and somehow, my eyes. My fear gradually evolves into awe and wonder as I realize the being made of gold in front of me, is me.

It's my own reflection in the now still water. I had been desperately mining for gold, when all along, I was made of the gold I sought. I had been chasing the momentary flashes and sparkles of gold in the stream, when all along, those flashes and sparkles had been coming from me.

Seeing that, I then slowly lift my head to gaze at the world around me. Everything—everything—the trees, the birds, the ground, the sky—is emanating the same gold. Everything was made of this gold. It's clear to me it had been all along. I just hadn't been able to see it until now.

I then woke up.

Distinguishing Fool's Gold from True Gold

This dream is our collective dream, the mass illusion that our egos perpetuate to maintain a sense of control. How easy it is to spend our lives in the pursuit of external acquisition because we mistakenly believe those things will bring a sense of happiness, fulfillment, and completion. And in the end, it doesn't matter what those "things" are. They could be the accomplishment of a certain milestone we deem successful, a certain salary, a certain achievement, a certain object, a certain relationship, etc. In reality, the only thing certain about any of them was that the happiness, fulfillment, and completeness we experienced from their acquisition was, at most, fleeting, and often not there at all.

The silt is our outer experience, and the mining pan is our own ego with its innate structural misperception of emptiness and incompleteness. We see how each pass through the silt is our ego chasing another transient promise from the world that this time the sense of fulfillment and completeness will be lasting and forever—only to lift the pan out of the water and see all the flecks and glints disappear. We see how it is only by putting the pan down and letting the water calm and be still, that we are able to see our own true reflection and know that what we seek is inside and not outside. We see how the gold is our own divine and undiminished essence, and our happiness, fulfillment, and completeness come from residing in this essence. We see how at first experiencing this essence can be frightening and disorienting, and can take some time to adjust to and grow into. Lastly, we see how it was only through experiencing and recognizing the gold inside that we could then look up and see it in everything around us.

The moment we connect with the gold that we are is the moment we connect with the gold that is everywhere.

When that happens—and it will happen if you are willing to let go of the mining pan, let the water be still, and see your own reflection—the possibilities available to you in the realization of your Soul Purpose will be well beyond what you could have ever planned or dreamed.

Effectively Using Both the Ego and the True Self

The journey of letting go of the illusions (fool's gold) of the ego for the real gold of the True Self illustrated in Kirk's dream takes courage. As Steve Jobs says, "Have the courage to follow your heart and intuition."

The second sentence of Job's quotation is equally important: "[Your heart and intuition] somehow already know what you truly want to become." He is essentially saying that there is a part of us that already knows. We have all experienced the truth of this. Whether we call that knowing instinct, gut feeling, or inner knowing, they point to the same thing. We suddenly find ourselves knowing how to move forward independent of our rational mind. But for most of us, those moments of connection are spontaneous and fleeting (and when they do emerge, we may be conditioned to not take them seriously). Rather than relegating these moments to lucky happenstance, we can more consistently and consciously connect with the part within us "that already knows" and avail ourselves of its wisdom, creativity, inspiration, and clarity.

The key is in effectively engaging both aspects, the ego and the True Self, in service to our Soul Purpose. How do we do that? We require three things:

1. We recognize these two distinct parts of our consciousness—ego and True Self.

2. We gain clarity on each of their functions and strengths.

3. We learn how to leverage the functions and strengths of both the ego and the True Self, utilizing each as they were intended.

Most of us are quite skilled at using the ego, which is the aspect of our consciousness that we rely upon most when navigating through life and the world. So, the real opportunity is to connect and align with the higher aspect of consciousness, the True Self, which is uniquely designed to provide inspiration, wisdom, and guidance in manifesting your vision of purpose and impact.

Have you ever heard the phrase, "I'm waiting for my dreams to come true"? Within this Soul context, this phrase is more accurately stated as *your dreams are waiting for you to come true.* In other words, your inner calling for greater fulfillment is a profound opportunity for you to step forward into this Higher Consciousness that is your True Self. Reawakening into this consciousness and residing in the loving, which is your essence, is the Soul's primary purpose. Additionally, this aspect of your consciousness knows the unique expressions of loving contribution that is yours to share with the world.

As you begin to fulfill your Soul Purpose, your life will be enhanced in two profound ways: 1) The experiential quality of your life improves as you reside more and more in the loving, joy, and wisdom of your True Self, and 2) your effectiveness and productivity tend to increase because you are showing up and making life choices from the clarity and wisdom of your Higher Consciousness.

Don't Judge the Ego

Now, at this point, we do have a caution. When people first discover that there are two aspects of consciousness—the ego and the True Self—and they learn of the majesty, clarity, and gifts that their Higher Consciousness provides and the negativity and stasis that the ego provides, there can be a tendency to judge the ego.

From our point of view, this would be an error in approach. The ego does have an important part to play. When functioning properly, it serves the True Self by implementing its guidance in the world. The difficulty comes when we identify solely with our ego, and we assign the ego roles and functions that it was never designed to fulfill.

So, let's take a closer look at how the ego and True Self function and the roles they play to support you in moving forward with your Soul Purpose.

The Function and Role of the Ego

The ego is comprised of the mind and emotions. Its main job is to support us in functioning in this physical world. A large part of its job is to keep us safe, which is clearly very important. It is the ego that reminds us to look both ways when crossing the street, take our vitamins, put on our seatbelt, go to work, write the grocery list, etc.

The ego, however, is not the best at discernment. It sees everything in black and white, as life or death. In its attempt to keep us safe, it will ring the inner alarm any time it perceives a possible threat. So, it is committed to keeping us in its "home turf," which is the comfort zone—that place where it *perceives* there is safety, security, familiarity, and control.

How does it support us in staying in our comfort zone?

It does so by creating mental images of the worst-case scenarios, conjuring up stories of failure, or running self-judgments when we consider change that it perceives as a threat. Experientially, these can sound like inner "*dis*courage" messages: *Play it safe. You're not ready. Other people achieve their dreams, not you. You'll never find your purpose. You're too busy. You don't have enough time or money. You're not confident enough. You're not smart enough. You're not skilled enough. You're not worthy. What if you get it wrong? You're going to fail. You're going to look like a fool. You'll ruin your reputation. You're being irresponsible. You're going to let your family down. This is going to be a disaster.*

Any of these sound familiar?

Again, the ego is not wrong or bad. We need an ego to function in this world. But when we identify fully as our small self or ego, we allow that aspect of our consciousness to run the show, which can result in never taking the risks required to grow, to go for our dreams, and to live a life of purpose and meaningful contribution. Being fully identified with the ego can also block us from receiving wisdom, clarity of purpose, as well as greater levels of support and guidance. These qualities are essential components of discovering and fulfilling our Soul Purpose.

The great news is, as we said earlier, we are much more than our ego or personality.

The Function and Role of the True Self

We established earlier that the True Self is who we truly are and is well equipped to provide us with the Northstar Intention for our Soul Purpose, as well as guidance in the journey. That is because the True Self functions as a conduit of Divine Love, Wisdom, Inspiration, and Creativity.

In contrast to the ego's messages, when we connect to our True Self, we will only hear "*en*courage" messages: *Follow your heart. You know. You are innately worthy. You are Love.*

When we connect and reside in our True Self, we are free of the conditioning and restrictions of the ego—free of the negative future fantasies, stories of failure, discouragement, self-judgments, and limiting beliefs.

When we consider that the root of "courage" comes from the French word *cœur*, or heart, it is fascinating that the ego offers messages that *dis*courage (*dis*- meaning "apart" from the heart), and the True Self provides messages that *en*courage (meaning *in* the heart). Thus, we arrive at another tool, a linguistic compass for our journey. When we are residing in the heart-centered loving of our True Self, we are "on purpose." Conversely, when we are identified with our ego and caught in its limiting beliefs, judgments, and emotional turbulence and separated from our heart, we are disconnected with our loving and "off purpose."

Steven Pressfield, author of *The War of Art*, in his follow-up book, *Turning Pro*, expresses it like this: "Our job, as Souls on this mortal journey, is to shift the seat of our identity from the lower realm to the upper, from the ego to the Self."

A Real-World Story: A Midlife Renaissance

When Jesse Gros, one of Licia's former students, was a young man growing up in California, he had an epiphany where a vision of his Soul Purpose came into laser-like focus. Suddenly, he could see himself on stage helping people and leading treks to give them opportunities to explore sacred places on the planet and in themselves. He began to dive into his dream and turn it into a reality, but then, in his words, "…I got scared—I felt I was too young and not prepared. I put it on hold. For 10 years on hold. During that time, I built a dam around my dream. That dam was filling every day I denied it, and my ego began to build a big story about why I wouldn't let the water flow."

Jesse went on to be successful, as society defines it. He worked as an insurance adjuster for a major insurance company, yet he began again to wonder about his dream and why he had become so disconnected from it.

To be very clear here, we want to express that from our perspective, there is nothing less purposeful or less meaningful and honorable in being an insurance adjuster than any other vocation. Those in the profession perform an important role in helping people during challenging times—a valuable service in this world. The point we are making here is that it simply wasn't Jesse's dream. The work did not align with his inner calling and Soul Purpose, and he was becoming increasingly aware of it.

One day, he was on a roof measuring the hail damage on a house that had weathered a storm. He had recently heard of two adjusters who had fallen from rooftops. With that, Jesse asked himself what might have been the most important question he could have asked in his journey to Soul Purpose: "If I were to die tomorrow, would I have been satisfied with what I did in my life?"

Jesse's answer to that question was that no, he would not, and that led him to renew his quest to realize the vision he had as a young man. He had heard of a master's program in Spiritual Psychology at the University of Santa Monica, which offered as part of its curriculum an opportunity to engage in a project to actualize a lifelong dream. He enrolled thinking that would provide him the structure he needed to create what he had in his heart.

What Jesse wasn't aware of at the time was that the true purpose of that project was to create a "force function" to have people confront and shed all the conditioning around who they truly were and what they were truly capable of in order to realize their dreams. To truly create what was in his heart, he had to shed the barriers his ego had placed between his vision and himself. In Jesse's words: "I took those two years to dismantle a lie—to dismantle the big story I had developed as to why I hadn't been going for it."

Jesse's "big story" consisted of multiple self-limiting beliefs, including:

- "Only very, very special people get to do what they love and be paid well for it. I don't think I'm that special."

- "I am not worthy of that kind of success."

- "The sacrifices will be too great."

- "I judge myself as too often changing directions in life, so I need to stick to what I am doing."

- "I should be further along than I am in order to do something like this."

Jesse did the work of letting go of these ego-created barriers and thereby came in greater contact with his own True Self. In making that contact, he saw his dream was 100 percent available to him should he dedicate himself, his intention, and his actions to its actualization. Today, Jesse owns a company, Insight Adventures, where he takes people to places like Machu Picchu in Peru and the summits of Nepal and shows them how to use their experiences to see the true, pristine, and golden reflections of their own True Selves.

And Jesse isn't stopping there. He describes his connection to his Soul as a connection that keeps upping the ante on new things to take on and experience. Jesse's Soul Purpose is not about a quest for one thing but about being open and embracing whatever comes forward that brings him alive. In his words: "People talk about having a 'midlife crisis.' I am feeling quite the opposite. What I am experiencing right now is a midlife renaissance. It's about being present to life, Soul, and spirit. Every day, how do I restore that sense of innocence, vitality, and possibility?"

Soul Purpose Practice

Creating and Living Your Northstar Intention

As we mentioned at the beginning of this chapter, a Northstar Intention is the intention you create to more fully connect with and manifest your Soul Purpose.

The following activity will support you in first connecting with the love, encouragement, and wisdom of your True Self. From that space, you will take a first pass at your Northstar Intention. We say "first pass" because creating a Northstar Intention is an evolutionary process. You do not need to pressure yourself into creating the "perfect" or "right" intention. This is just the first step. We encourage you to revisit and refine your Northstar Intention as you gain more awareness of your Soul Purpose.

Take some time with the following activity, including writing your responses in your journal.

1. To begin, connect with love of your heart. This is a portal to your True Self. Many people find it is supportive to place their hands on the heart, or to think of someone, including a pet, that they love dearly. Allow that experience of love to fill you.

2. As you reside in that space of loving, gently explore what you sense as the essential calling of your True Self. In other words, what is being called through you into the world at this time? Whatever shows up is fine. Allow yourself to explore. There is no right or wrong, no better or worse, response. You may want to ask your heart or True Self—that loving sense within you— to share further about your calling. What wisdom, inspiration, or guidance does your heart or True Self have to share?

3. Given your responses to the questions above, create an intention for living your Soul Purpose

more fully. As you develop your Northstar Intention, infuse it with your enthusiasm. Below are examples of some Northstar Intentions:

a. My intention is to honor my Soul's calling by (include your Soul Purpose here).

b. My intention is to be open to new possibilities, inspiration, and guidance in service to my Soul Purpose: (include it here).

c. My intention is to easefully connect with and reside in my True Self as I (include your Soul Purpose here).

d. My intention is to joyfully open myself to my journey of Soul Purpose and the revelation, growth, and inspiration that are available to me.

4. Read your intention aloud. What do you experience when you read and hear your intention? How does it sound to you? Be present to the quality of your Northstar Intention. Is it uplifting? If you experience it as "flat" energetically, that is a sign you have an opportunity to further refine it, imbuing it with language that inspires and uplifts you.

5. When you feel complete with the process, acknowledge yourself for your devotion to your Soul Purpose and unique contribution to the world.

We encourage you to post your Northstar Intention in places where you will see it daily, so that it remains actively present in your life. You can also use your Northstar Intention as an antidote when you experience discouraging messages from your ego. Rather than taking in and giving more attention to these messages, use Step 1 of this activity to reconnect with your heart and True Self, and state your Northstar Intention to yourself or out loud.

Additionally, we recommend you periodically set aside time as you have now to revisit and refine your Northstar Intention.

Bonus Round: Tracking the Ego and the True Self

If you are curious to gain more awareness of the two aspects of consciousness—the ego and the True Self—we encourage you to make the following activity a part of your Soul Purpose Practice. You're going to need to unpack your linguistic compass for this one!

1. For one day, be present to the messages you're hearing within. Remain in neutrality as you observe yourself. Resist the urge to move into judgment, which will only reinforce your identification with your ego.

2. Throughout the day, when you become aware of inner discouraging messages, ask yourself the following: What are the messages? Which part of me is speaking? Which messages do I hear most frequently (my ego's "favorite hits")? How do I feel emotionally and physically when I listen to those messages? Am I connected to my heart?

3. Throughout the day, when you become aware of inner encouraging messages, ask yourself the following: What

are the messages? Is there a particular encouragement that I hear more than once or that I experience as the primary message? Which part of me is speaking? When I listen to these encouragements, how do I feel, both emotionally and physically? Am I experiencing myself as connected to my heart?

4. At the end of the day, write down your responses in your journal.

5. What insights into your inner territory has this practice provided you?

6. What are ways that you can continue to use your linguistic compass to support staying "on purpose"?

7. Acknowledge yourself for your willingness to devote time and energy in service to your self-awareness and Soul Purpose.

LIBERATION

CLEARING THE BLOCKS
THAT KEEP YOU STUCK
SO YOU ARE FREED TO SCALE
THE SUMMIT OF SOUL PURPOSE

CHAPTER 3

CLEARING UP THE MYTHS OF THE PATH

"The day came when the risk to remain tight in a bud was more painful than the risk it took to blossom."

—ELIZABETH APPELL

To illustrate the dynamics of risk, let's go back to the wonderful metaphor of the plant created by Elizabeth Appell (often attributed to Anais Nin), but let's go deeper. Literally deeper. Let's go deeper to a seed under the ground—a bougainvillea seed resting within the soil of a hillside.

Life isn't bad for the seed. It is surrounded by moist warm soil. It is comfortable. Things have not changed at all for a long time, giving the seed a sense that it has its surroundings under control. Sometimes it dreams of growing into more. Of moving upward. Of seeing what might exist beyond the moist warm soil, and what, in that new space, it might be able to be. It has a sense that inside itself is a code—a greater purpose to become something spectacular—something that feels amazing and at the same time is in greater service to its world. But it doesn't know for sure, and it doesn't know what exists up there. In the meantime, it is moist and warm here.

The Illusion of Control and Safety

The truth is, those conditions are transient and the sense of control an illusion. The truth is, if the seed stays there as a seed, any of the following will eventually happen. A flood could wash the soil and seed away. A bird could peck the seed right out of the ground. A fire could rip through the hillside and singe the seed. The seed has absolutely no control over those things.

Let's imagine the seed has an enlightened moment and sees all this. It is willing to venture up into the unknown to see what it can become. It must then allow its shoot to break through its shell and casing to begin the journey upward and realize what once provided comfort and safety has become an anchor holding it back from the fulfillment of its Soul Purpose. Soon, that shoot breaks from the earth and leaps into the sky, exploding outward like fireworks full of purple and red blooms to feed the bees, birds, and become home to all manner of animals. It has learned that in taking the risk, it experiences an exponentially greater expression of who it truly is and its capacity to serve a glorious and waiting world. It has learned that what it thought was bringing it safety and value was holding it back from the experience it was born to have. It now truly feels its Soul Purpose.

As we look at our lives, where are we reflecting the experience of the seed? What are we seeing as "the risk" as we contemplate moving toward our Soul Purpose? What are we seeing as necessary items for safety and comfort that we might have to "sacrifice"? What might we need to liberate ourselves from in order to go all in toward what brings us alive? Is it the status of a role? Is it the revenue of our current default occupation? Is it a community or family that might not understand and criticize or reject us?

To borrow from Jesse in the previous chapter: If you were to die tomorrow, would you be happy that you held back from the experience of finally breaking free of the earth and leaping into the sky?

The Ego—The Guardian at the Gate

As we shared in the introduction, the second pillar of the Soul Purpose Method is Liberation. This phase of the process is designed to support you in clearing those blocks that prohibit you from: 1) connecting with your True Self, 2) clarifying your Soul Purpose, and 3) taking aligned action to more fully manifest your unique contribution in the world.

What are these blocks? They are mental blocks—limiting beliefs, stories, and judgments—as well as the negative emotions that accompany them.

Let's return to the Soul Purpose Method Formula.

Intention + Liberation + Co-creation ⇨ Soul Purpose

The process of Liberation represented in the formula is about identifying and clearing mental and emotional blocks. This requires us to work with the aspect in our consciousness that functions as the guardian of these blocks—our loyal companion, the ego.

As we explored in the previous chapter, the ego's job (from its perspective) is to keep us safe. In fact, we could consider the ego our internal Senior Vice President (SVP) of Risk Management that works 24/7, with no vacation or sick days, to maintain us in our comfort zone. It does this by scanning our thoughts, choices, and actions for anything that it perceives as threatening.

Therefore, whenever we are considering a change, the ego perceives this as a potential threat to the status quo and the security and safety that status quo provides. This is completely understandable because change brings growth, a requirement of which is stepping outside of our comfort zone.

At those times, our loyal SVP of Risk Management (a.k.a., ego) is right there sending messages of *warning, steer clear, it's too risky!* As we explored earlier, these take the form of discouraging messages that block us from making the choices and taking the actions required to live our Soul Purpose. They even prevent us from considering we have a Soul Purpose!

Some of these messages are so widely held that we have deemed them Soul Purpose Myths. In our work with ourselves and others, we have identified seven of the most common myths that keep people from connecting with and living their Soul Purpose. As you review each of these, consider the ones that you most relate to.

Seven Soul Purpose Myths

Myth 1: *I don't have a purpose.* We addressed this myth in the opening of this book when we shared the "biggest secret" is that your Soul Purpose is already within you.

We all share the ultimate Soul Purpose to learn, grow, and love. The expression of that love can take an infinite variety of forms. Consider your activities from this last week. What did you do—no matter how small—to support another person? Did you provide comfort when needed? Share a smile or friendly compliment? Take the time to be there for a friend, child, parent, sibling, spouse, coworker, supervisor, client, neighbor, or stranger? For the most part, we take these actions for granted, as simply part of our daily lives; however, they and hundreds of actions like them are part of the fulfillment of our Soul Purpose.

This truth was beautifully demonstrated at a Soul Purpose workshop we led with a Fortune 500 company. We facilitated a group creating a personal Vision of Impact. At one point, the participants were invited to stand up and share this vision. One person at the support level of the organization stood up and shared,

> The truth is, I am not in a position where I can directly impact product and process design, but that really doesn't matter because what brings me alive in this world is simply bringing joy to people. I recognize from this workshop that joy and happiness can impact everything, and so my Impact Vision is to do something in every meeting I attend that helps bring joy and happiness to the people there. I know that will impact everything they do and create.

She was 100 percent correct. Her Impact Vision would, at the very least, improve the day of her coworkers and could play a part in fostering an environment conducive to the creation of innovative products that would enhance the lives of millions.

Myth 2: *I have to find or figure out my purpose.* This myth is similar to Myth 1 in that it is based upon a misunderstanding of what our Soul's purpose actually is. The ego assumes it must be something grand and singular for it to be a "real" Soul Purpose. That may be true for some. However, as Myth 1 explains, for many of us our Soul Purpose is expressed in a myriad of ways, from brief acts of kindness to lifelong acts of service and contribution.

The second misunderstanding that forms the basis of this myth is that a Soul Purpose must be "found" as if it were a hidden or lost object that had to be uncovered. The predominance of this myth is really one of the main reasons we wrote this book. Your Soul Purpose does not need to be found because it is not "out there." It is not outside of you. Rather, the opportunity is to connect with and reside more consistently in your True Self—that aspect of your consciousness that is fully aware of your purpose and path on this planet. It is right here waiting for you *because it is you.* The real work is to disidentify with the ego, release the limiting beliefs and stories that block you from that ego identification, and realign with your True Self, which already has the clarity, inspiration, and guidance you need to align with what you are here to do. This book and its activities were designed to support you in that journey.

Myth 3: *I don't have enough money, time, and/or opportunities to pursue my purpose. Once I do, then I'll be* *able to focus on and fulfill my purpose.* This myth is a wonderful way the ego keeps us from stepping forward in any action that will take us out of our comfort zone. This myth perpetuates a story that we are dependent on outside circumstances to live our Soul Purpose. When we recognize that any loving act serves as a fulfillment of our Soul Purpose, the inaccuracy of this myth becomes self-evident. However, what most people mean by this is that they do not perceive that they have the external resources necessary to take the big leap out of their current job or life circumstances into an occupation (paid or not) that has heart and meaning for them. We like to respond to this common concern by sharing this excerpt from a commencement speech given by actor Jim Carrey:

> So many of us choose our path out of fear disguised as practicality. What we really want seems impossibly out of reach and ridiculous to expect, so we never dare to ask the universe for it. I'm saying, I'm the proof that you can ask the universe for it….My father could have been a great comedian, but he didn't believe that was possible for him, and so he made a conservative choice. Instead, he got a safe job as an accountant, and when I was 12 years old, he was let go from that safe job and our family had to do whatever we could to survive. I learned many great lessons from my father, not the least of which was that you can fail at what you don't want, so you might as well take a chance on doing what you love.

Life holds no guarantees. The ego would like us to think that if we play it safe, we will be safe. That is simply not true. This illusion is made evident when we consider how often unexpected life circumstances occur—accidents, illnesses, losses, layoffs, economic shifts, and much more.

Please understand that we are not advocating taking foolish risks. From our experience and our work with others, we have found we can take steps and "lean into" new choices as a series of experiments. Often when we do, we open ourselves up to unexpected surprises that support us in the fulfillment of our intention. In contrast, staying stuck and playing small can keep us from the flow and bounty available to us outside of our comfort zone.

Myth 4: *I'm not sure the purpose I've identified is my real purpose. What if I'm wrong? I don't want to make a mistake.* If you have been reading each of these myths in sequence, by now you are probably catching onto how the ego plays this game. Once again, this myth is based on the misunderstanding that there is a single, "right" purpose that we must find, else we make a grave life mistake. Can you hear the multitude of discouraging messages in that? *You must be right, or you will make a mistake.*

In actuality, the very act of learning and growing regardless of outcome fulfills your Soul Purpose. It is inherently a path of experimentation and discovery and can be a glorious adventure of growth and transformation. As we begin to realize that anything we do will at a minimum provide us with incredible opportunities to grow, there can be no mistakes, only lessons. There is no right or wrong, merely experiments and adjustments.

Imagine if a toddler held the ego's perspective that he must walk correctly, or he would be wrong and make a grave mistake. He would never rise off his knees and take one step! The pressure would be too great. Our path of Soul Purpose is very similar to a toddler's process of learning to walk. But rather than walking, we're learning how to awaken into the love that we truly are and live from that awakened state.

Myth 5: *I'm not "good" enough (confident, patient, focused, disciplined, skilled, smart, gifted, motivated, or energetic enough) to pursue my purpose.* This myth is based upon the misunderstanding that we should already be at a certain level of accomplishment or ability in order to pursue our goals and dreams. As we discussed in the previous myth, our path of Soul Purpose was designed to be an avenue for our learning and growth. That is this path's primary intention.

A high IQ, giftedness, even self-confidence are not required. What is required is willingness. Willingness to step out of your comfort zone. Willingness to traverse unknown territory. Willingness to make self-honoring choices despite the voice in your head telling you that you are not good enough. And finally, willingness to do the work to release the dominance of that voice so you can first connect with and then more consistently reside in your True Self.

Myth 6: *I have too many other responsibilities, obligations, and priorities.* This myth calls to mind the old adage, "If you want something done, give it to a busy person." We all lead full and busy lives. From our experience, that doesn't change, though the activities filling those busy lives do. Often, as we take our first steps along the path of Soul Purpose, we continue the activities and work of our daily lives. For example, the following famous writers held day jobs as they were fulfilling their creative callings:

- George Bernard Shaw, telephone company employee

- Arthur Conan Doyle, surgeon

- Kurt Vonnegut, police reporter, public relations writer, and car salesman

- Margaret Atwood, barista

- Charlotte Brontë, governess

There is also the possibility that your Soul Purpose is not about adding a new endeavor to your life, but about how you are approaching the endeavors you're already engaging. In later chapters, we will cover how to set small, doable goals as part of your Soul Purpose Action Plan. The idea is to honor yourself whether you are getting started on a new vision or embracing the way you are already showing up within yourself and in the world.

Myth 7: *I can't let down or alienate people in my life. What would they say?* In some ways, this may be the most difficult myth because it speaks to one of the most common fears—the fear of rejection. As you will read in the following real-world story, one client held strong concerns that her company and its leadership would be critical of her if she dared to share her heartfelt goals of meaningful social impact. Her story is an incredible demonstration of what can happen when we are willing to let go of our self-imposed limiting beliefs, including our ideas of others' critical reactions. In her case, it was more than a happy ending; it was miraculous. Her inner success and fulfillment were reflected in her company's increased profits and product line.

But that isn't a guarantee. It is not uncommon for those around us to be the outer picturing of our own ego's attempts to keep us small. In essence, they become the second line of defense to keep us in our comfort zone. Their messages may come from a loving intention to guide or protect us (just as our ego's messages do), but they can act as discouraging messages nonetheless. Ultimately, it is our choice as to which voice we will follow—the one that supports us in playing small and staying "tight in the bud" or the one that supports us in residing in the majesty and freedom of our essential nature.

The Risk in Daring to Live on Purpose

The seven Soul Purpose Myths can be boiled down to this: If I go there, I have to leave here. And I'm not sure there is better than here. So, is it worth the risk to leave here? Here isn't the best thing. In fact, I'm pretty dissatisfied, but it feels comfortable, familiar, and safe. I feel in control here. I'm not sure that will be the case there. It's just not worth the risk.

This is the ego's perspective.

Because we all have egos, we all will run some version of these myths and limiting beliefs in our minds—no matter how subtle. It is part of the human condition. An intrinsic part of our process of growth is becoming more aware of our mental blocks and consciously liberating ourselves from them.

A common reaction when we first discover these blocks is to judge them and the ego for using them "against" us. As we mentioned earlier, this is an error in approach. Why? Because judging them fuels the very thing we want to release. When we judge these limiting beliefs and our egos for running them, we judge ourselves. These self-judgments are just another set of limiting beliefs that compound the issue and block our freedom. Can you see how this process ultimately results in us staying in the same cycle of limitation?

Rather than becoming self-critical, frustrated, or discouraged, the opportunity is to accept all aspects of ourselves as part of our human experience. Then, go about the business of releasing mental blocks and replacing them with more empowering beliefs.

On the path of Soul Purpose, we have the sacred opportunity to sacrifice the constructs that keep us playing small. We let go of the illusion of safety, comfort, and control. We release ourselves from playing inside the lines. We risk living outside the lines in a much vaster reality. That may sound good to us, but it can be terrifying to the ego. Waking up is understanding that the only real risk is to stay where we are—to not take the risks that provide us with opportunities to grow, honor ourselves, and experience our greater and more authentic nature.

As synchronicity would have it, while writing this chapter we came across this quotation by author Randy Komisar that powerfully sums up the real risk in playing small and ignoring the inner calling to live our Soul Purpose: "The most dangerous risk of all—the risk of spending your life not doing what you want on the bet you can buy yourself the freedom to do it later."

A Real-World Story: To Bloom Where One Is Planted

Claire attended one of our Soul Purpose workshops. She is the Global Lead of Design for a Fortune 500 toy company, and she came to the workshop with a quandary.

Claire had a strong vision of Soul Purpose—to use her life for the empowerment and well-being of the underserved, marginalized, and invisible—but she couldn't imagine how she could fulfill this inner calling in her current position and at her company.

She came to the Soul Purpose workshop hoping that she would get clarity on changing careers as well as the support to do so. But what she discovered was entirely different. She examined her assumptions and discovered her dilemma was based on perceived risks that she saw when looking at her position and the company:

- *The risk to her reputation.* She had taken 20 long years of hard work and dedication to become known as a highly talented yet business-minded design leader.

- *The risk of rejection.* She worried that putting forward the belief in the success of products that could serve those populations would be thought of as unrealistic and that she personally would be perceived as losing her business or profit-oriented focus.

- *The risk of her team's reactions.* She worried that her own team would not believe in this radical new vision and lose their faith in her as a leader.

- *The risk of failure.* She had concerns that if the endeavor moved forward, it would fail miserably once out in the world and thereby dampen the industry's move toward positive-impact products.

As Claire began to truly examine these perceived risks, she discovered more accurate interpretations of reality that illuminated her perceptions of risk as potential myths.

As she looked more deeply at the risks one-by-one, she became aware that though her fears felt real, the beliefs she held out of fear had no basis in objective reality. With that understanding, she was able to open to new possibilities and to consider her current situation with fresh eyes:

- There was always the risk of rejection, regardless of what new line she would put forward.

- There was no guarantee that any line she created would succeed, and what's more, the company was getting increasing feedback from the market that something new was needed.

- A deeper look into her team indicated that she'd get more faith and respect by trying something new for positive impact, even if it failed.

- Taking personal responsibility for how the entire world of business might react to positive-impact products (should her line fail) just wasn't realistic.

- Lastly, she recognized she was judging the leadership as unable to appreciate a positive-impact line of products, when in truth she had no evidence that was accurate.

All this drew the realization from Claire:

Instead of feeling like I needed something new to make a difference and connect with my personal purpose, I may actually be able to do exponentially more good from right where I was. There was a moment of knowing that was magical. Seeing that what lights me up personally is in alignment with the goals of the company I work for and the work I do changed my life. I went to work on Monday morning and literally everything looked different to me.

Seeing through fresh eyes inspired Claire to make the self-honoring choice of staying with and bringing new ideas into her company to serve her Soul Purpose, rather than leaving her position to try to create another endeavor.

Over the last few years, through her connection to her own Soul Purpose, Claire has created products that are more and more oriented toward social impact. Many of them have become the brand's greatest drivers of business success with one pro-social line, actually imagined before the workshop, shifting four years of steep decline into a seven percent increase in global sales. We think it is important to note that Claire ended up creating a successful business strategy for her company by fulfilling her Soul Purpose Intention to improve the lives of kids. It is important to recognize that, contrary to the ego's story, we can do good *and* do well. Continuing with us as a coaching client, Claire designs products that remain prolific, including lines representing people with disabilities and other disenfranchised groups in society. In the end, the impact Claire had on the business and the culture of the brand was such that when she proposed an internal program to bring this Soul Purpose work to the entire design division of the company, it was enthusiastically received.

We then had the privilege, in an internal company workshop, of joining Claire in facilitating her 60-member team to connect with their True Selves and inner callings to make meaningful contributions. Here are what some of those participants said:

"I had never known about the ego and the authentic self. I had always thought all those negative thoughts and the 'I can't do that's' were actually me—not just my thinking. Seeing that, I can now choose to let those thoughts go and choose new thoughts that fuel my creativity and productivity."

—A team member

"A lot of you know me as kind of a control freak, but what this exercise we just did united me with, is that it is probably safe for me to let go a little—to spur more creativity by 'allowing' rather than 'pushing.'"

—A team leader

"A lot of you don't know this, but when I design a toy, I am thinking of a young child who may be lonely and may be plagued with self-judgments about who they are, and that perhaps I can give them moments of freedom from that. From this last exercise, I see that in a lot of ways I am still that child inside, and in letting go of my own self-judgments and limiting beliefs, I will be able to create even more powerful moments for these children that perhaps can free them as well."

—A senior designer

Soul Purpose Practice

Soul Purpose Mythbusters

Have you ever been astonished by a really good magic trick? It appears real until you see how the magic trick is executed. Once you know how it works, your initial wonder at the "magic" dispels. You see the trick for what it actually is—a well-performed illusion. Similarly, it is easy for our egos to convince us that these myths are real as long as we don't examine them too closely. Once we see how they are being used, the trick loses its power because it has been revealed as the illusion that it truly is.

The following process will support you in identifying and exploring those myths that your ego has used to maintain the status quo and keep you in your comfort zone. As you become more aware of the patterns running in your own consciousness, you will be able to recognize your own limiting beliefs as the well-performed illusions that they are. This is the first step in releasing yourself from these myths so that you can adopt more empowering truths.

Set an intention to reside in the qualities of openness, curiosity, and neutrality as you write down your responses to the following in your journal:

1. Review the seven myths described earlier in this chapter. Which myth(s) jump out as the most familiar? Which do you catch yourself saying the most, either to yourself or to others? Which *seem* to be the most true, real, or legitimate in your life?

2. Once you have identified your ego's favorite myth(s), take a few minutes to explore how each is used to keep you in your comfort zone. How do each of these myths keep you blocked? (Note: Each may do this slightly differently by creating confusion, impeding clarity, justifying procrastination, perpetuating a sense of inadequacy or unworthiness, etc.)

3. Now, allow yourself to consider the possibility that these myths are not real. What if they are merely thoughts? What if they are simply mental tricks or illusions performed by your ego to keep you safe and in your comfort zone? How would this change how you relate to these myths?

4. What are other more positive thoughts that you could hold about yourself and your ability to live your Soul Purpose? List them in your journal.

5. What are the positive outcomes that may occur from holding this new, more empowering perspective? How might these support a greater connection with your Soul Purpose and the actions you could take to more fully step into it?

6. Acknowledge yourself for your willingness to identify and liberate yourself from these common myths and mental blocks.

CHAPTER 4

RELEASING THE BLOCKS TO LIVING IN PURPOSE

"Everything you want is on the other side of fear."

—JACK CANFIELD

In the last chapter, we explored myths and mental blocks that are common when taking the leap to live our Soul Purpose. Now as we continue our process of Liberation, we will turn to the negative emotions associated with these mental blocks.

What underlies most of these mental blocks is a fundamental and universal kind of human experience: fear.

The secret to moving beyond fear and other common negative reactions comes down to two things: first, our willingness to dig underneath, discover, and dismantle the illusion (a.k.a., the specific underlying myth) associated with the negative emotions, and second, our choice about how we relate to ourselves and our feelings.

The story that follows is a true story that transpired many years ago between Kirk and his then five-year-old son, McKinley.

Fear Is Part of the Path

It happened at Gillian's Wonderland Pier in Ocean City on the Jersey Shore. McKinley surveyed all the rides as he would whenever he first arrived. This time, his eyes stopped on the ride that had always terrified him—the log flume. He watched intently as the logs made their way up to the precarious top, teetered there in the turbulent stream, and then fell and fell and fell still farther into the misty darkness of the hidden pool of water. The riders' screams drowned out even the cacophony of the other coasters, twisters, and merry-go-rounds. McKinley's look remained unaltered. Nothing else existed for him at that moment.

"I want to go on the log flume ride," he announced.

I couldn't have heard right—he was only five, and he'd always been terrified of that ride. "Hey, McKinley, usually when we get up to it you decide not to go—and that's okay. It's kind of a big boy ride."

"But I want to. I really want to, Daddy. Really."

"Well, okay, when we get over there, you can still change your mind. It's okay, you know?

He didn't answer. My words passed through him the way water passes through a strainer that refuses to waste its function on inconsequential things.

We arrived at the base of the ride. I suddenly realized that the height requirements as represented by the smiling plywood gopher in front of us are the perfect way for a proud five-year-old to save face. But instead of shrinking and perhaps bending his knees a bit to ensure the legal mandate of rejection, I see McKinley stretch every joint and tendon from the tip of his middle toes to the top of his scalp. His feet angled absurdly to stand on their sides and his neck somehow managed to pop out another inch from nowhere.

Now, he and the gopher were eye to eye.

"McKinley, just because you're tall enough doesn't mean you have to—"

"Daddy—you need to stop now—I want to go on it." (When my son wanted me to hear him, he used my words: "You need to stop now.")

I acquiesced silently, but not without trepidation. I crawled into the cramped cockpit, and McKinley crawled in between my legs. I was about to try to remind him again that it was not too late to stop, but my words were cut short by a cold metal safety bar that clanked down upon us, sealing my words and both of us into the compartment. I felt McKinley's little sharp fingers dig into my arms. We began to move and both knew there was no return now. I couldn't give him a way out because there was none.

The log boat bounced against the sides of the steel flume, the water getting more turbulent. My son's fingers tightened more.

Fear was pouring in now. His fingers dug even deeper into my skin, he pushed harder back into my chest trying to somehow escape, and he yelled through his tight jaw, "I didn't know about this part, Daddy. I'm scared."

I knew this part was nothing. We were not even close to the scary part. We had not even begun the ascent—the slow, methodical inching upward toward the top of the tallest point before falling down the waterfall. If he was scared now, what would happen in just a few minutes? Fear gripped me as well. If I was not even able to comfort him now, what would I do then? What was I thinking in letting him ride this?

Suddenly, the giant steel hook engaged the underbelly of the log and violently yanked us out of the water and relentlessly pulled us up the ascending steel track. My son suddenly saw what was coming, and he wanted none of it. His sharp little fingers dug deep, deep into my arm, and he tried to climb over the bar. I pushed him back between my legs. He began to panic.

"Oh no, Daddy, now I know why I hate these things so much!! I hate it! I hate it! I hate it! Daddy, I'm scared—I want to get off, Daddy, I want to get off. Now Daddy, now!"

His panic did not let up. We were climbing higher and so was the pitch of his voice. There was nothing in my bag of dad-tricks for this. So I did all I could do: I gave my own fear of not knowing what to do over to a Universe willing to take it and share it with me.

The Universe replied: "Why don't you simply be honest, Kirk? Why don't you be as honest with McKinley about what is happening as you can possibly be?"

I had no idea what to do with that, but I had nowhere else to go. I broke down the reality of the situation as simply and honestly as I possibly could: "McKinley, you're supposed to be scared. They make the ride so that you'll be scared. Especially right here. Especially this part. They make the ride to be scary for us on purpose."

When he heard that, something changed in him. I felt his sharp little fingers relax slightly. He gulped mouthfuls of air, and his voice was still quivering when he asked, "I'm supposed to be scared?! They make the ride on purpose to be scary, Daddy?!"

He seemed totally bewildered. I had never considered that he might not be aware of this. But, of course, he would not be. Everything in the life of a five-year-old was meant to be fun, not scary. The feeling of fear for him at that moment could only mean one thing—something must be wrong for him to feel this way.

"Yes! Yes, McKinley! They make it on purpose that way! They say, 'hey, let's make a ride that little boys like McKinley and big boys like Daddy will be scared on, so they can tell stories later! And here we are on the scary part!"

And with that, as we got to the top of the incline, the panic evaporated from my son and up into the salty air of the Jersey summer. Not the fear, but the panic. The fear remained, but in a form that was natural and acceptable to him—a form that came from his new awareness that this was the part of the ride, the part of life, when we were supposed to be scared. The ride we were on was designed to be scary at times. Knowing that made all the difference to his experience of the ride.

Before the giant fall downward, the log flume made a gentle and meandering half-circle high up in the sky over the boardwalk. We could hear the approaching waterfall, and I worried that McKinley's panic might return upon hearing and seeing what lay ahead. Just then, he turned so I could see the side of his face and asked me his last question before we were to plummet downward together.

"So Daddy...I can be scared sometimes...it's okay to be scared sometimes?"

"Yes, little man, it's okay. It's okay."

The waterfall was a roar now. McKinley's sharp little fingers did not dig anymore, but firmly and calmly held mine tightly. The nose of our log began to dip into the misty abyss and plummeted. I felt McKinley's head gently lean back for the first time to rest squarely on top of my chest. The pounding of my heart seemed to make things familiar to him. It sounded just like his in that moment, and he stayed there as we fell and fell and fell still farther.

Our impact at the bottom caused a wave to engulf us, and we emerged as wet as newborns freshly fallen into the waiting hands of the world—which is what we were in that moment—newborns screaming the way newborns do.

To our left, sitting on a bench was his grandfather, grandmother, mother, and brother. McKinley was already with them, his hand up, way up, collecting high-fives as if they were big ripe apples hanging just for him.

Fear Can Signal an Opportunity for Growth

What this story of a moment between a father and a son illustrates is that fear is simply the feeling that accompanies our human experience when we are sitting on the crest of something new and unfamiliar. To feel fear does not mean that something is wrong but that the future holds something we simply cannot see or understand yet. The fear can signal a passage to places rich with opportunities for growth. Often, it is also the part of the ride that we experience as scary.

Like McKinley, we may misunderstand the fear as a sign that something is wrong. Then, we mistakenly make the feeling of fear itself wrong instead of recognizing it as a powerful beacon letting us know we are on target for our next great adventure, where our Soul Purpose lies.

McKinley's story demonstrates the courage, or strength of heart, it takes at times to venture into new terrain outside of our comfort zone. This journey beyond what is familiar and comfortable is a requirement for growth and expansion; therefore, the fear that accompanies it, while not enjoyable, does become a known companion on the journey. As we become more familiar with the terrain of growth, we enhance our skills in traversing it. We also diminish our resistance to it, which is itself a significant source of mental and emotional suffering. In other words, the more we practice, the easier it gets.

So, as we look into the unknown and feel fear, the question is: Will we pretend to be too small to take it on, or will we stretch every joint to claim our true size so that we might bravely enter the ride toward our Soul Purpose? Will we realize it's just the ride and meant to be scary at times? Will we move forward anyway, emerge into our Soul Purpose like newborns, and rise to grab the apples there just for us?

There is another lesson that we can draw from McKinley's experience. Before the ride, both father and son lived within a more limited reality. You may have already recognized a variation of Myth 5 ("I'm not good enough") at play: "I'm not old enough," "He's not tall enough," "We're not courageous enough."

The beliefs and attitudes that both McKinley and Kirk were running created mental blocks. The emotion associated with these blocks was fear. This is the same emotional thread that often weaves through the seven myths and other mental blocks.

In McKinley's world, that fear was all-encompassing. It even compelled him to try to escape, an action that could have produced disastrous results. Thankfully, Kirk's inner guidance provided him with a way to effectively address his son's fears, and McKinley, who trusted his father's guidance, was comforted enough to move through his fear and experience success.

Effectively Working with Fear When It Arises

The roles that Kirk and McKinley played in this story are no different than the ones we play when we consider going for our dreams and living a life of greater meaning and purpose.

The egoic aspects within us that are scared are often expressions of younger aspects of our consciousness. Just like in McKinley, they can be comforted by the wiser, more mature, and compassionate aspects of our consciousness.

Yet how often do we react to our own fear with negativity and judgment? Imagine if, rather than responding to his son's fears with caring and reassurance, Kirk had been harsh and condemning. Or imagine if he had allowed himself to remain in his own sense of limitation and had matched McKinley's fears. How might that have reinforced both of their self-imposed limitations?

The path of Purpose is one that often exists outside of the comfort zone. Therefore, a key opportunity on this path is to gain greater self-awareness and skill in working with the parts of the personality or ego that become upset or anxious as we venture into new terrain.

As we face the fear of the unknown and triumphantly move through it, like McKinley, we free ourselves from our outdated stories and reclaim our true nature and the life of joy, love, and purpose waiting for us.

How do we effectively address fear? As we stated in the opening of this chapter, one way is to identify and dismantle the illusion that underlies it. As we let go of the mental blocks—the myths and other limiting beliefs we have held as real—the accompanying emotional upset goes as well. This is because emotions follow thought. In other words, negative beliefs trigger negative emotions. Conversely, positive beliefs create positive feelings.

However, sometimes the emotions that get triggered can feel more intense—even all-consuming. If we explore these feelings more closely, we may discover a quality about them that feels more childlike—much like McKinley's response in the earlier story.

Why are these feelings so childlike? Fear and other negative emotions that we experience in adulthood sometimes have much earlier antecedents. These younger aspects in our consciousness represent opportunities to bring acceptance and loving to parts of ourselves that hold issues still unresolved or incomplete. Like Kirk, as we respond to these frightened younger aspects with compassion and caring, we can bring resolution to these issues and dissolve the mental and emotional suffering that block our progress.

Another interesting observation about these younger aspects in consciousness is that their fear is often based on their assumption that *they* have to face the scary situation alone and be in charge of it. Not only is this inaccurate, but it is also ineffective. These younger parts of us are not prepared to effectively handle adult-level situations. (No wonder they are so scared!) That is our job—the adult consciousness—as the leader of our life. Once this misunderstanding is communicated and cleared up, the fear often dissolves.

Licia had her first, powerful experience of this many years ago. She explains:

Early in my career, I had the opportunity to meet a prestigious psychologist who lived and worked in Manhattan. Being young and a new visitor to the city, I was completely outside my element and comfort zone. I was meeting a woman who was highly educated and well respected and ran a successful practice in the Upper East Side of the city. Who was I to interview her?

But that was exactly what was scheduled. As I prepared for the meeting, I could feel the anxiety rising within me. I was a neophyte, a novice who hadn't even earned a degree in psychology yet. I felt so small and incompetent.

As a master's student in Spiritual Psychology, I had recently learned about younger inner aspects and how to work with them. That's when it occurred to me that the fear and inadequacy I was experiencing felt very young. I realized that it wasn't the "adult me" having these reactions; it was a younger aspect inside of me. When I tuned into the fear and what part of me was running it, I sensed a little girl around five or six years old. I began to talk to her in a gentle, loving way, just as I would a real five-year-old who was frightened. I reassured her that she didn't need to lead the interview. In fact, if she wanted to, she could "stay home."

When I suggested this, the immediate sense I felt was relief and a decrease in fear. That indicated to me she liked this idea. I imagined her sitting in a comfy chair where she would hang out with her favorite dolls while I travelled to interview the psychologist.

Encouraged by this inner interaction, I took it a step further. I asked if there was an aspect of my consciousness that was excited by the prospect of meeting the psychologist and felt skilled in interviewing. To my delight, there was! I then took a few minutes arranging for that inner aspect to be the one who took the lead. Immediately, I felt a surge of enthusiasm and empowerment.

I walked to the psychologist's office with a spring in my step. I felt totally different. My anxiety and timidity had transformed into self-confidence and enthusiasm. I believe this energy radiated out from me because I noticed that strangers on the street were pausing to notice and smile at me as I passed—certainly something that is not my usual experience, particularly on the bustling streets of New York City!

The interview went very well. The psychologist and I had a great time together. But the big win for me was that I had discovered a way to effectively address my fears by caring for the parts of me that were holding them. I continue to use this technique to this day.

A Real-World Story: From Retiree to Rock Star

Like Kirk, Licia also has experienced a family member liberating himself from his mental and emotional blocks. In her case, her husband, David, recently made this profound shift.

David's love of music started in his childhood and never stopped. Singing in his church choir and taking piano lessons as a boy grew into starting his own garage band as a teenager and then touring the country as a young man. His parents weren't too keen on their beloved son risking his financial welfare on his dream of being a musician. They encouraged him to get a college degree, especially since he had been awarded an engineering scholarship, and secure a "real" job. To them, music could be a wonderful hobby while he earned a good, steady salary in an established profession.

Though he initially ignored their entreaties and left college to become a full-time musician, he never forgot his parents' admonishments. After several years of being on the road and playing in a variety of clubs and bars, he grew tired of the shadier side of the music industry and got a job as an engineer in a Fortune 500 corporation. As his parents had predicted, his love of music was relegated to hobby status. His myths of not being good enough and not having the resources that he needed were reinforced by a nine-to-five job that was less than satisfying.

Fortunately, David discovered the power of identifying and releasing his limiting beliefs and the negative judgments, attitudes, and emotions associated with them. Recognizing his relationship to music needed healing, he devoted an entire year to clearing up his misunderstandings, self-judgments, negative attitudes, and emotional upset. As he freed himself from his mental and emotional blocks, his lifelong love of music re-emerged and with it a growing conviction that he was no longer willing to stay in a job that was not interesting or fulfilling.

But the very thought of leaving the financial security and benefits of his engineering career triggered concern and fear. He and Licia would be facing an immediate 50 percent reduction in their household income. Thoughts of "I don't have enough money" (Myth 3), "I've got too many other responsibilities" (Myth 6), and "I can't let down people in my life" (Myth 7) loomed large. The two worked individually and together to release the limiting beliefs and comfort those parts inside that felt afraid.

Near the end of that year of inner work, David mustered the courage to write and submit his letter of resignation. Within 48 hours of informing his supervisor, David received an email out of the blue from an earlier music partner, Michael Landau. Michael is a Grammy Award–winning guitarist, who is revered internationally as one of the top musicians in his genre. David and Michael hadn't spoken for over 10 years! Yet within just two days of David taking action on his dream, Michael was reaching out. When later asked in an interview what prompted him, Michael shared that he had "just woken up one day with the thought of getting back together with David and starting a new musical project as partners." Needless to say, David and Licia were both flabbergasted! They both knew the power of this work, and here was the proof once again.

The happy ending didn't end there. Within one week of David leaving his position, he received unexpected news that he, Michael, and two other world-class musicians were being booked on a European tour, where they would be playing many prestigious clubs. Additionally, he and Michael recorded an album together on which David wrote the lyrics and performed lead vocals on many of the songs.

At the time of writing, they have toured Asia, with a second European tour scheduled for next year, as well as the completion of their second album.

Now, rather than dreading going to work, David wakes up each morning in gratitude, joy, and wonder at the life that he is living. His relationships to himself and to his creative expression have transformed into a new story of success—one in which he is flourishing both internally and externally as he shares his love of music with the world.

Soul Purpose Practice

Releasing Mental and Emotional Blocks

Liberation and true empowerment come from effectively clearing our mental and emotional blocks, and compassionately working with the aspects in consciousness that hold them. The following practice will support you in experimenting with and having a direct experience of this powerful approach:

1. Based on the previous exercise, select the myth that shows up most frequently for you. For example, let's say you select Myth 5—"I'm not good enough."

2. Set an intention to be aware when this myth shows up in your day. It may show up in relation to your Soul Purpose, or it may show up as a reaction to other people or situations in your life.

3. When it does, note your reactions. What limiting beliefs show up? What are you feeling emotionally and physically? For example, if you chose Myth 5, you may notice a persistent belief of "I'm not smart enough to handle this situation" and feelings of overwhelm associated with it.

4. Now, rather than judging those reactions, which keeps you stuck in them, neutrally observe and accept them. Recognize that they (and you) are not wrong or bad. They are simply mechanisms by a caring ego that is doing its best to keep you safe by its definitions.

5. Bring acceptance and compassion to that part of you that wants to keep you safe. Some people find that placing their hand over their heart or belly supports them in connecting with themselves in a caring and reassuring way. Share messages of acceptance, understanding, reassurance, and compassion with yourself silently or out loud. For example, "It's okay," "I accept myself," "I forgive myself for judging myself as not smart enough,"

"I forgive myself for running this limiting belief against myself," and "I appreciate and accept all parts of me."

6. Check in again. How has moving into acceptance and compassion shifted your inner experience? Are you noticing any difference in how you are relating to these thoughts and beliefs or to yourself?

7. Now as you did in the Soul Purpose Practice in Chapter 3, replace the limiting belief(s) with more empowering ones. You can do this by completing this statement: "The truth is that (fill in new empowering belief)." For example, "The truth is that I am a beautiful and capable human being, willing to learn and grow." Or, "The truth is that I have handled previous challenges with intelligence, tenacity, and resourcefulness, and I'm fully capable of doing so now and in the future."

8. Acknowledge yourself for your willingness to try something new in service to your learning and growth.

Bonus Round: Another Approach for Clearing Emotional Blocks

As both Kirk's and Licia's stories showed, sometimes the path of growth can activate intense, negative emotions. Fear can often point to young inner aspects getting triggered. Both stories also illustrated how effective it is to respond with love, compassion, and patience when these younger aspects arise. At these times, we become the caring parent, comforting and taking charge. In the following process, you will have an opportunity to practice this technique for yourself:

1. Set an intention to be aware when concern, anxiety, or fear show up in your day. These emotions may show up in relation to the topic of your Soul Purpose, or they may show up as a reaction to other people or situations in your life.

2. When they do, take a moment to pause. Take a deep breath and note your reactions. What thoughts are running that are causing the anxiousness? What are you feeling emotionally and physically?

3. Now recognize that these reactions are not the totality of you. They come from the ego and those aspects in your consciousness that have been triggered.

4. See if you can sense if the fear is coming from a younger aspect inside that is seeking comfort and solace. If so, bring caring, compassion, and acceptance to this part. You may even want to put your hand on your heart or over your belly to create a more loving connection. As you would a young child, reassure this aspect. It is not alone, nor does it have to take the lead in the situation that it fears.

5. What would that inner aspect like to do instead? Mock up its ideal situation in your imagination. Continue working with that aspect until you experience the anxiousness diminishing and being replaced with relief or calm.

6. You can choose to complete your process at this point by sharing your gratitude and love for that younger part within and to yourself for self-care.

7. Or, if you'd like to continue further, you can check inside to see if there is another aspect that would be beneficial to use as an ally in the situation. This is an inner aspect that feels enthusiastic and confident in its ability to assist you in this situation.

8. Ask the new aspect how it can support you. Listen within to see if you receive any responses. These responses may come as an inner voice, pictures, or simply a sense of a creative approach.

9. Check in again. What are you experiencing now? Are you feeling differently? Are you noticing any shift in how you are relating to the situation and to yourself?

10. Acknowledge yourself for your willingness and devotion to yourself and your growth.

CHAPTER 5

CHOOSING THE INNER LEADER FOR THE VISION

"The intuitive mind is a sacred gift, and the rational mind is a faithful servant. We have created a society that honors the servant and has forgotten the gift."

—ALBERT EINSTEIN

Now that you have learned how to identify and clear the mental and emotional blocks that can keep you stuck and playing small, it is important to learn how to designate the leader inside of you.

Inner Leadership: The True Self and the Ego

Imagine a snake and a lizard in the middle of a vast sandy flat desert. Off in the distance is a beautiful butte, abruptly breaking the plane and towering thousands of feet high into the sky. A conversation between the lizard and the snake ensues in which they both confess to being curious about what it might be like on the top of that butte. At one point, they look at each other and jointly commit to heading off on an expedition to find out.

As they move side by side over the sand of the desert expanse, the snake finally stops and confesses to the lizard that he can move a lot faster than he currently is. They confer, the lizard jumps on the back of the snake, and off they go, zipping across the sand as only a snake can.

Soon they bump into the granite face of the towering butte. The snake does his best to continue, but each time he tries to ascend the cliff face, they both tumble down to the desert floor. The snake was not made to climb cliffs; it was made for the flat and open sand.

Then, the lizard has a thought. After many, many miles whipping across the desert on top of the snake, it had totally forgotten its own legs and claws. It explains to the snake that while the snake was not made for the wall of granite, the lizard surely was with its four legs to spread out and find the edges and cracks for its sharp claws to fit into. With that, the snake gently took the tail of the lizard in its mouth, and the lizard began to scale the vertical expanse like only a lizard can. There would be occasional times when it would still need the snake and would whip it to one side or another to wrap itself around a rock or root to aid their passage up, and then the lizard would resume, taking them both to what seemed like the top of the world.

When they arrived there, they took it all in. They could see everything from an entirely new perspective. The junipers and cacti that once towered above them were now green specks splashed across the endless brown tapestry of sand. The hawks and buzzards that once hunted them from above were now safely below them. They saw the zig-zag track the snake had made for miles across the desert floor as it headed toward the butte and where it suddenly stopped and was replaced by the marks of the lizard's claws that had brought them to the summit. They saw that the key to their ascent had been their willingness to switch from master to servant when the direction and dimension of their journey had changed.

From Flatland to Rise

The companionship and collaboration of the snake and the lizard are no different than those of our ego and True Self. As we become more aware of the pitfalls of the ego on our own ascent, it is tempting to make the ego "wrong" or "bad," or, even as written occasionally in spiritual texts, to want to "kill the ego." But once again, this does not serve our Soul Purpose.

The truth is, the ego or personality has been useful in our life when it is functioning at the level it was designed for, which is to navigate the physical level. In the parable of the snake and the lizard, this level is the vast two-dimensional "flatland" of physical reality. In physical reality, it is useful to know when to go left or right, to recall how to get to the store, to remember our phone number, to know how to balance a checkbook, or to develop a business plan for our big vision. The key here is not to get rid of the ego but assign it the role for which it is best suited.

That role becomes evident when we finally arrive at the vertical butte of our Soul Purpose and awakening. Then, like the snake trying to scale the granite face on its own, the ego is simply not the best one for the job.

If we look closely, we will quickly notice that the ego applies its sense of left and right to this new dimension and comes up with "right" and "wrong." It applies its sense of addition and subtraction to this new dimension and comes up with, "I'm shining too bright" and "I'm not enough." It's not trying to be destructive; it is just looking at this new world through the only eyes it has—flatland eyes that can only see and project a dualistic paradigm.

Who Do We Let Lead?

When our intention in life begins to look upward on the vertical axis of the inner and not just the flatland of the outer, then the question becomes: What do we do? Do we dispatch with the ego altogether (pretending for a moment that we could)? Or do we learn from the snake and lizard's arrangement? If we encounter the ego drowning out the intention of the True Self, do we create a new dynamic where the True Self becomes the master and the ego its servant? Do we let the True Self, which holds no fear, doubt, resistance, or constriction, be the master who generates and explores what brings us alive and develops the bold vision of what we might bring to this world? And do we let the ego be the servant who generates the report on what pitfalls there might be (which the True Self can use or not use), figures out the logistics, maps out the way forward, and follows through on the plan?

In Licia's personal story, this choice came when she heard the very clear voice of her True Self sharing with her that she was not crying from sadness but from joy. In that moment, she connected with her True Self and allowed its inspiration, clarity, and vision become the leaders for the next era in her career. Once this shift happened, her decision to resign was evident (as was her haircut to mark the decision). However, the implementation was done in cooperation with the ego. It was her ego that took care of the details: scheduling a meeting with her supervisor, submitting her letter of resignation, and then completing the many tasks associated with setting herself up as a business consultant.

You can look at each of these aspects' roles in whatever way fits your life. Is your True Self the inner CEO and the ego the SVP of Risk Assessment? Is your True Self the architect and ego the builder? Or, as one filmmaker coaching client recently exclaimed during a session, "I get it! My True Self is the director, and my ego is the producer!"

There are a myriad of ways to model this, but it all comes down to having reached the place where the only way forward is up, and up requires the part of us that has travelled the terrain, that knows up, that *is* up.

As we dare to switch the ego's role from master to servant and move from the familiarity of the flatland to imagine the possibilities that lie on top of the butte of Soul Purpose, we realize that only our True Self is equipped to ascend.

Now that you have begun to clear the blocks to your Soul Purpose and to liberate yourself from the limitations of the ego, you have come to the place in your journey where you are now ready to ascend.

At this point, the key opportunity is for both the ego and True Self to function in the ways for which they are best suited: the True Self as your inner CEO, the part of your consciousness well equipped to be the leader of your unique vision of Purpose, and the ego as your inner producer, well equipped to take action in physical reality. The opportunity is to acknowledge and utilize the contributions that both the ego and Self provide.

We can live an inspired and inspiring life—a life of meaningful contribution and impact—through the cooperation of the ego and the True Self. The process includes attuning to the True Self, receiving its inspiration to birth our vision, and utilizing the ego to implement that vision in the world.

When both aspects work together as intended, an amazing thing happens. The constraints of the ego fall away, and the True Self shines forth. We have had the privilege to witness this miracle hundreds of times with those who we have supported. In each case, it is a personal renaissance that becomes the portal to a life of greater inspiration, joy, meaning, and fulfillment.

A Real-World Story: Pounding Swords into Plowshares

A few years ago, a coaching client shared his conundrum. Sam Polk was successful on Wall Street, but he experienced a crisis of conscience, left Wall Street, and after a many-year spiritual walkabout, landed in South Central LA and started a nonprofit called Feast to help connect families with healthy food and nutrition habits.

During the conversation, Sam confessed that while the nonprofit was fulfilling to a degree, there was a part of him that wanted out but that he was scared to let it out. That part of him was the "killer businessman"—the one that thrived on Wall Street. From that place, he was thrilled at the prospect of building a business, overcoming obstacles, jousting with and beating the competition, taking on the giants, making a healthy profit, and experiencing entrepreneurial success.

When asked why he was scared to let this aspect of himself out, he described what had happened "last time." Back on Wall Street, he didn't like what he had become. He felt ashamed at the choices the "killer businessman" had made. Now he was confused and tormented. He was experiencing a growing inner calling but fiercely judged that part of himself as dark and perhaps even evil.

Here was a clear example of Myth 7 ("I can't let down or alienate people in my life") functioning as a block to Sam's Soul Purpose. In Sam's case, he was afraid the "killer businessman" inside of him would hurt others by putting profit over people.

Sam was trying to move forward into his calling, but his inner CEO at the time was his ego. Oriented in the flatland of "left or right" and "good or bad," his ego judged the businessman inside Sam as "bad," blamed it for Sam's Wall Street experience, and rang alarm bells whenever it would raise its head.

The coaching helped Sam pull apart the two things he had combined, which happens a lot in the two-dimensional flatland of the ego. Sam separated the "killer businessman" from the events, choices, and consequences, he had experienced on Wall Street.

Sam was then asked, "Now that you have separated the part of you that really brings you alive—the amazing businessman within you from *how that inner businessman was used* in that old experience—what new perspective comes forward?"

With that distinction in mind, Sam was able to see this aspect of himself without judgment. He left the flat desert floor and started his way up the vertical face of the butte. In that moment, he replaced his ego as his inner CEO with his True Self and was now able to look at the situation from that elevated place. His True Self held an entirely different perspective:

> The killer businessman in me isn't "bad"—it can actually do a lot of good. If I apply its energy and vigor in the same direction as I have my nonprofit, I will be harnessing this very powerful and authentic part of me in service to what is currently my purpose in this world. What if there was a self-sustaining business model to support healthy food in urban "food deserts" where there is currently only fast food?

Over the next months, Sam let his "killer businessman" out. With his True Self as inner CEO steering his Soul Purpose Vision and his ego working out things such as business models, store concepts, and supply chain dynamics, Sam was able to open an innovative restaurant concept called Everytable that enables those living in urban neighborhoods to purchase healthy and delicious meals for at or below the price of fast food.

What started as one Everytable location has become a chain of seven at the time of writing, with thousands of meals served. Sam's "killer businessman" is doing everything that brings Sam alive—building a prolific for-profit enterprise, taking on the giants, and doing good in the world. Sam is experiencing the miraculous things that can happen when the True Self is master and the ego is servant, as are the thousands of people who are now getting healthy food where there wasn't any before.

Soul Purpose Practice

Discovering the Genius of Your True Self

Poet David Whyte speaks of the awakening to one's essential nature in this way:

> We speak of genius when we speak of leadership, hoping for some of that elusive genius in ourselves, but the word genius in its Latin originality means simply, the spirit of a place. The genius of Galapagos lies in its being unutterably itself; the genius of an individual lies in the inhabitation of their peculiar and particular spirit.

David has uncovered a profound truth: your True Self is your genius.

You may not be fully aware of all your unique qualities and how innately capable and ready you are when you show up in your true nature. The next two processes are designed to support you in discovering that truth for yourself.

Part One: Who Inspires You?

We will start by identifying those qualities that you most admire. Who inspires you, and what about them is so inspiring? Set an intention to reside in a place of curiosity and honest exploration as you answer the following questions.

1. Who most inspires you?

2. What about them inspires you? What behaviors, actions, attitudes, and/or choices do you admire most?

3. What qualities of the True Self do you see them embodying?

4. Which of these qualities do you admire the most?

5. Review your answers, particularly the qualities that you listed. Select three to five of the qualities that most inspire you, that you admire the most. List those qualities.

6. Now for the good news! Those qualities that you listed, which you most admire in another, are within you! That is because:

We can only see in others what already exists in ourselves.

If you see it in others, you have it inside. In fact, you could not see it in others, if it's not inside of you. Any time you see and admire someone else, you are seeing a reflection of an aspect or a quality within yourself. In psychological terms, this dynamic is called a positive projection.

Often, though, it does not feel that way. Often, what we see in others seems nonexistent or unattainable within ourselves. Psychologist Piero Ferrucci explains this common phenomenon:

> Instead of owning, so to speak, the transpersonal qualities which are beginning to infuse their being and therefore expressing them in their lives, some people may take a much easier though less rewarding course: They may attribute these qualities to another person—a guru, a therapist, a public figure, a friend, or the like....Meanwhile, they are able to maintain the status quo in their own lives, although they are depriving themselves of precious gifts.

However, once you discover this key—that whatever you admire in another is a reflection of you—it opens a doorway to your True Self. In part two of this process, you will have an opportunity to experience the truth of this dynamic for yourself.

Part Two: Recognizing and Owning the Qualities of Your True Self

The process of identifying and owning positive projections is one of the most powerful keys to liberating yourself from patterns of self-doubt and self-limitation. Rather than attributing the qualities of leadership exclusively to others and disowning the best within yourself, you can disidentify from your ego's perception of you and disconnect from its patterns of fear, doubt, and limitation. This liberates you to experience the majesty of who you truly are. As you come into greater contact with your True Self, you are able to live from a place of higher altitude, inspiration, love, and creativity in alignment with your Soul Purpose.

We both learned the following process as graduate students at the University of Santa Monica. To this day, it remains one of our favorite approaches.

Set an intention to reside in the qualities of attunement, connection, and inspiration as you answer the following questions:

1. Briefly review your responses from Part One of this process:

   a. Who most inspires you?

   b. What about them inspires you? What behaviors, actions, attitudes, and/or choices do you admire most?

   c. What qualities of the True Self do you see them embodying?

   d. Which of these qualities do you admire the most?

   e. Select three to five of the qualities that most inspire you, that you admire the most.

2. If it is true that we can only see in others what we have within ourselves, what is your mirror reflecting about who you truly are?

3. Are you willing to take responsibility for more fully accepting these qualities within you? If yes, what does that mean for you?

4. Embrace the positive projection, reside in those qualities within you right now, and let them speak. What wisdom and inspiration do they want to share? We encourage you to speak aloud as if the quality is speaking directly. For example, "I am Creativity. I infuse (your name) with brilliance and inspiration. I am…"

5. The wisdom and inspiration that you have just shared (and heard) is an authentic expression of who you truly are! This is the voice of the visionary inside you. Are you willing to embrace your True Self?

6. Are there actions you could take that would be a living demonstration of your True Self and its qualities, wisdom, and inspiration? These actions can be in support of you owning this aspect of your consciousness, or they can be in support of you stepping forward in your vision of Soul Purpose. Note: You do not have to commit to these actions. In this process, you're simply considering them. Write down any possible next actions you are considering.

7. Take a few minutes to review the actions you wrote down, and add any further actions, inspirations, wisdom, or guidance that you received in this process.

8. Acknowledge and appreciate yourself for owning those qualities of your True Self and for exploring inspired actions in support of your Soul Purpose.

CHAPTER 6

REPLACING LIMITATION WITH AUTHENTIC SUCCESS

"Everything you need to be great is already inside of you.
Stop waiting for someone or something to light your fire.
You have the match."

—DARREN HARDY

I n the last few chapters, we have explored the mental blocks (a.k.a., limiting beliefs and judgments) and the negative emotional blocks as part of the identification with the small self or ego. Left unchecked, these blocks create what we could call our "Story of Limitation," meaning the story we tell ourselves, which unknowingly can keep us stuck in a default life.

In this chapter, we will take a closer look at this Story of Limitation and its dynamics with the intent of replacing it with a new Story of Authentic Success—our Soul Purpose Vision.

What Story Are You Telling Yourself?

If you ask most people what has created the story of their lives, they will likely recite a series of circumstances that happened to them, not of their making or in their control. Their perspective of reality could be described as: My life happens as a result of external circumstances in which I am a bystander. As opposed to: My life happens as a series of experiences that I am intending, believing, choosing, and acting on as my reality.

If this scenario sounds "woo-woo" to you, let us show you that there is nothing woo-woo about it. Imagine these scenarios:

Person A wakes up one morning and has the momentary thought they'd love to start a business that brings high-quality and healthy meals to poor and challenged neighborhoods. Their very next thought is, "I know nothing about food, restaurants, etc.—who am I to even think about this?" And then they dismiss the whole notion and go back to sleep. Their life continues as usual, and they wonder why nothing ever changes. They continue to feel lethargic and unfulfilled.

Person B wakes up and has the same thought and the same next thought of failure. But then they entertain a third thought: "Just because I know nothing about this right now doesn't mean this is something that I can't do." They lean into it. Learn. Stumble. Learn some more. Stumble some more. Have a win. Have a failure. They eventually discover a system where the same food is sold for a little more in an affluent neighborhood so that it can be sold for less than fast food in the challenged neighborhoods. Three years later, they are sitting on a chain of seven stores with another five in the works, and thousands of people are eating healthier as a result.

What distinguishes the first and the second person and the story of each of their lives from that morning on? Was it a series of circumstances that happened to randomly befall each of them, or was it the story they each chose for themselves? The first person chose a story that what they didn't currently know, they couldn't do. The second one chose a story that what they didn't currently know, they could lean into, explore, and learn.

Two Stories, Two Results—Both True

You may have already recognized this story as Sam's from Chapter 5. In the real-world story, Sam played Person B.

The more effective choice is clear from the example. But how many times have we unwittingly chosen the path of Person A? If we are not paying attention, it is easy to choose a Story of Limitation, and from the core belief of that story, no new possibilities can be generated and, therefore, no new experiences can be enjoyed. The belief—*Who am I to even think about this?*—does not create new possibilities.

Fortunately, Sam chose what we call a Story of Authentic Success. Through his application of the Soul Purpose Method and his own dedication to his healing and growth, he liberated himself from the mental and emotional blocks that were his previous Story of Limitation, awakened into the truth of who he was, and chose a new story for himself that aligned with that truth. From the core belief of his new story—his Soul Purpose Vision—new possibilities emerged and with them new experiences. The belief—*Just because I know nothing about this right now, doesn't mean this is something that I can't do*—allowed for the emergence of countless new possibilities and experiences.

Both stories can come true.

What is key is that:

Whichever story you choose will come true.

As we take a closer look at the dynamics of each story, we see that there is nothing "woo-woo" about it. The two stories illustrate the mechanism of creation: What we intend, what we believe, what we choose, and what we act on will create the story of our lives. The challenge is that for many of us, the beliefs we have generated about ourselves are so deeply ingrained that we mistake the beliefs writing our story for laws governing it.

As a result, so many of us are living a default Story of Limitation when we could be living a Story of Authentic Success.

Two Potential Traps in the Story of Limitation

The benefit of choosing a Story of Authentic Success rather than a Story of Limitation is evident. Yet, just like the myths and limiting beliefs we explored in Chapter 4, our Story of Limitation is often not obvious to us. If we are not aware of our Story of Limitation, we can fall into two additional traps.

Trap 1: Relegating our past as the "old" Story of Limitation

It's easy to judge where we have come from and criticize the approaches we have previously used. Do you see how clever our ego can be in creating just another, subtler variation of the same limiting story? The truth is our experiences have led us to being here.

In our coaching practices, we frequently use the metaphor of stepping-stones across a river. Each stone plays a role in getting us to the next one; one is not less significant than another, regardless of where it appears in the order.

Instead of condemning our past actions, we can review them as a series of life's "stepping-stones." We can see that each of our experiences—our victories and defeats—played an important part in our learning and growth. Each has prepared us to step forward into a whole new level of authentic success, into living our Soul Purpose, more fully.

Trap 2: Imposing our Story of Limitation on our Soul Purpose Vision

If we are not vigilant, we can also fall into another trap. We may mistake progress for setbacks.

How might this show up? Let's return to Sam. He could have spent time developing an inspired Soul Purpose Vision of bringing healthy meals to challenged neighborhoods. Enthused by his vision, he may experience some initial progress, but somewhere along way he would bump up against challenges, which are an essential part of the learning and growth process. If he were still running a Story of Limitation, he might interpret these challenges as evidence that he is not capable enough or that his vision is a pipe dream. He might become discouraged, even give up, rather than see these challenges as feedback from the Universe—opportunities for greater healing, learning, growth, and possible refinement of his Soul Purpose Vision.

Fortunately for Sam, he did the inner work necessary to release his Story of Limitation, comprised of myths, limiting beliefs, and self-judgments. He embraced and cultivated a new Story of Authentic Success for himself that supported his inner calling and Soul Purpose Vision.

If you have been engaging with the activities presented in the earlier chapters of this book, you are well on your way to identifying and replacing your Story of Limitation with a new Story of Authentic Success. In the activities at the end of this chapter, you will have the opportunity to acknowledge the journey that got you here and equipped you for the next phase of your journey—developing and co-creating your Soul Purpose Vision.

In the next real-world story, you will meet Serene, who unwittingly fell into this trap, mistaking progress for setbacks. Fortunately for her and for all who she eventually served, she recognized that her old Story of Limitation was playing and recommitted to living her new Story of Authentic Success.

A Real-World Story: Mistaking the Miracle as the Disaster

Serene, a coaching client and the CEO of a 300-person company, was midway through our work together when she arrived at a session quite exasperated. She described a situation that had suddenly emerged:

> I think we're in real trouble. Yesterday, two of my leaders came into my office and announced they were leaving. They are starting their own business. They might be taking some clients with them. The people here and other clients are going to think something's wrong with the company or will lose faith, thinking all the good people might begin to leave. Then we'll lose all our great talent and, with them, our clients and be out of business. This is really bad. This is not what I had planned at all.

Serene had real fear and urgency in her voice, which was totally understandable given she had built her company from the ground up with hard work, dedication, and diligence over a period of 10 years. While absolutely understandable, the story she was playing inside herself was a Story of Limitation. It's true that losing two of her key leaders could be a significant challenge, but what Serene had started to create was a series of fictitious dominoes that, despite *feeling* quite real to her at the time, were still based on a complex web of hypothetical events far from her current reality. Bringing this to Serene's attention was helpful and slightly calming for her, but there was something much bigger and more important going on that would move Serene into an entirely different place inside.

Just a couple months earlier, Serene had created a new vision and singular intention for the kind of company she wanted hers to become. It was a powerful vision. Serene had also started a nonprofit for social impact and suddenly saw how both her company and her nonprofit could come together under one purposeful mission to connect people to the resilience and strength of their own True Selves. She had begun to make changes in alignment with her vision and share those shifts internally.

Sometimes in conversation, she would speak to her leadership and openly express her concern that they may not be aligned with where she wanted to go. She frequently got feedback like, "But things are going fine, why change anything?" and "Let's not rock the boat; we have something that's working. Let's keep her steady as she goes" that would deflate her enthusiasm.

Just then in the session, when Serene was reminded of these previous conversations, she suddenly stopped and looked off into space as if seeing those moments from a whole new perspective. Her face turned from expressing fear, to gentle concern, to calmness, to a blossoming vigor.

She began to speak, "Wait a second. This isn't bad. This is great. They were never really on board with where I wanted to go. I guess inside I always knew that eventually, for this new vision to really come to fruition, I would need to separate from them. Now, they are simply walking out the door, giving me room to bring new people on board who are more aligned with our new purpose-oriented mission, which means I won't have to keep pushing. These new leaders will be building this place in that direction totally on their own and bringing ideas to it that I haven't even thought of yet. Their energy will attract more great people and clients who are also aligned. This isn't bad. This is the best thing that could have happened."

Armed with the vision and intention she had generated just a couple months before, Serene was able to see the events transpiring in a new light. The Universe wasn't conspiring against her, it was conspiring *for* her in accordance with the vision and intention she had so clearly given it.

In that moment, she had dismantled her Story of Limitation and replaced it with a Story of Authentic Success. That new story fueled a myriad of possibilities emanating from her True Self and subsequent actions planned and executed through cooperation between her True Self and ego. What resulted was the positions being filled with new, purpose-led, invigorated leaders. The right people had suddenly appeared, and the company went on to become a much more purpose-oriented enterprise, staffed by highly enthusiastic and aligned people, which attracted more invigorated projects and clients. The choice to let go of her Story of Limitation for a Story of Authentic Success allowed Serene to replace her inner attitude of constriction and depletion with one that embraced and created expansion and possibilities.

At the time of this writing, Serene's vision continues to produce amazing results. Recently, instead of simply providing marketing services for one of her clients, she is inspiring them toward social impact initiatives. And the results have been remarkable.

Additionally, just a few days ago, she shared a video taken in Asia, where over a hundred children in a schoolhouse built by her nonprofit are cheering her on with her husband standing by her side.

Soul Purpose Practice

Creating Your Soul Purpose Vision

Rather than falling into trap #1 (relegating your past as the old Story of Limitation), the following process will support you in reflecting upon and recognizing the beauty and purposefulness of the journey that has brought you to where you are now. The more you utilize this approach, the more you can free yourself from the temptation to judge, criticize, or minimize the events, choices, and actions that comprise your past. Instead, you can acknowledge your outer accomplishments, as well as the inner resourcefulness, unique qualities, and gifts that you bring. With this greater awareness of yourself and your gifts, as well as your enhanced connection with your True Self, you are now more prepared to create the first iteration of your Soul Purpose Vision.

Set an intention to reside in the qualities of acknowledgement and gratitude, then write down your responses to the following questions in your journal:

1. What are the accomplishments and achievements that got you here? What are the inner resources, skills, qualities, and gifts that supported you in accomplishing them?

2. What are some of the challenges and obstacles you faced? What are the inner resources, qualities, skills, and gifts that supported you in overcoming them?

3. Now, slowly read aloud the inner resources, qualities, skills, and gifts that you have noted. As you speak these

aloud, really take them in. Be present with, receive, and own each of these inner resources, qualities, skills, and unique gifts as you. These have enabled you to arrive where you are today and will continue to be of great service as you move into this new paradigm of creation and purpose.

4. Take a moment to connect with the loving of your True Self. Allow this wise and loving aspect of yourself to share how the story of your life has always been a Story of Authentic Success.

5. Residing in the loving wisdom, openness, inspiration, and creative possibility of your True Self, explore the following questions:

   a. If you knew you could not fail, what type of life experience would be joyful and meaningful for you? Keep in mind, you are *not* committing to anything; you are simply exploring the possibilities. (Hint: If a part of you goes into "I don't know," then ask yourself: If I did know, what would I say about this? And just see what comes up. There are no right or wrong answers.)

   b. What would you be experiencing in your outer reality? How would you be sharing your loving, skills, and talents? What meaningful contribution would you be making in your world? Who or what would you be serving?

   c. What would you be experiencing in your inner reality? What does it feel like to share yourself and your gifts? How are you relating to yourself? How are you relating to others?

6. Allow yourself to reside as fully as you can in this vision of your life. Step into it as if it were happening now. What do you see, hear, smell? How are you feeling? What are you doing? Is anyone with you? What further inspiration and/or awareness come forward?

7. How does this vision of your life relate to your Soul Purpose? What new awareness of your Soul Purpose does this vision provide you?

8. From this inspired and self-honoring place, take time to write your Soul Purpose Vision. Know that this vision will evolve as you do, so there is no right or wrong. Trust yourself and what is showing up right now as an important part of the process.

9. Review your responses and vision, then acknowledge yourself for your willingness to create your Soul Purpose Vision—a new chapter in your Story of Authentic Success!

CO-CREATION

Working in partnership with Spirit
and the Universe all around you
to manifest your unique Soul Purpose

CHAPTER 7

ELEVATING FROM EGO CREATION TO CO-CREATION

"What you can plan is too small for you to live."

—DAVID WHYTE

Now that you have set your intention, freed yourself from blocks that keep you stuck, and reconnected with your True Self, you are ready to explore the third and final pillar of the Soul Purpose Method: Co-creation. This pillar will support you in moving from the flatland to the butte so you can more consistently reside in your True Self and manifest your Soul Purpose.

By now it is evident that the ego and True Self have vastly different functions and strengths, as do their methods of manifestation. Your connection with your True Self offers a portal into the inspiration, synchronicity, and grace that characterize the realm of conscious co-creation.

Force Versus Flow

Years ago, a student of ours named Mai Mai found herself on a whitewater rafting trip on the Salt River through the wilds of Arizona. Each morning, a different rider could get off the raft and have a kayak to themselves for a day. Mai Mai was incredibly excited the morning of her turn. She hopped in the kayak, grabbed the paddles, and off she went with the intent to meet the rafters at a rendezvous point by the end of the day.

Paddles in hand, she tried to hit the rapids just right, explore the tributaries, seek out wildlife, and make sure she experienced everything that was possible on the river.

In a short time, she was utterly exhausted. Blisters formed on her hands. Her arm and back muscles were cramping. What she imagined as an open, fun, and freeing experience was actually a lot of work, effort, and struggle. She reached the point where she just had to stop, lift the paddles out of the water, lean back, and rest.

In her profound weariness, she closed her eyes and let her heartbeat slow and her sweat evaporate into the dry desert air. After a bit, she opened her eyes. The scenery had changed. She wasn't paddling and yet she was moving quite swiftly. She became awake again to the reality that she was indeed on a river, flowing with a current much stronger than she could ever create using her paddles. In just the few minutes she had closed her eyes, the scenery had changed, and it hadn't taken any effort on her part.

Now Mai Mai left her eyes open. Still leaning back with paddles in hand and out of the water, she let the natural current of the water move her forward. Without her attention on the mad paddling—and what might she be missing—she was able to truly experience the river and the epic life of its waters and canyons: the too-many-shades-of-reds to count on the canyon walls, the diverse shapes of clouds bridging the lips of the cliff tops, an osprey diving like a kite caught in a downdraft only to disappear into the water and reemerge with a catfish. She heard the tinkling of a feeder stream gently falling into the edge of the river and the rare and almost unbearable silence when the water and wind were still, with only her own breathing breaching its perfection.

There came a point where Mai Mai put the paddle back into the water, but in an entirely different manner. It was no longer in a frantic flurry of flying in and out of the water to move the kayak forward. Now, it was gently submerged in the position of a rudder. Every now and then, Mai Mai would angle it slightly to the left or right, not to fight the current or force a direction that wasn't natural to the flow, but to use the paddle in cooperation with the current. That cooperation would guide her kayak to those things that caught her interest and curiosity, or to add just a bit more ease and flow through the occasional rapids that are a part of any river journey.

There and then came that blinding moment in which the river gave Mai Mai its lesson about life. Mai Mai realized that her true progress had not come from the force and ambition of her own paddling, but from the cooperation with the massive, unstoppable, never-weary, never-blistered, perfectly directed current of the river. Her experience of freedom did not come from conquering the current through paddling, but from surrendering to it—with one paddle gently submerged, making choices and actions in alignment with it, yet undeniably making her own unique path

This is Co-creation—the cooperative and symbiotic relationship we can choose between us (and the actions and choices we make) and the incomprehensibly powerful and limitless current of Spirit that flows all around us. On our journey to Soul Purpose, we may try to move against the flow of the current. We may also pretend our progress is all ours. Or, we can recognize the presence of our Soul Purpose, invite It in, and use Its power to create currents and flows that add grace, speed, richness, effortlessness, and enjoyment to our voyage.

Co-creating the Journey of Soul Purpose

Glorious possibilities open for us when we are willing to move from ego-creation to Co-creation. When we are willing to finally let go of the illusion that the frantic digging of the paddles in the water will manifest our Soul Purpose faster, we can lean back and let the immeasurably powerful and infinite possibility–laden river draw us forward. Our intentions, choices, actions, and expressions of gratitude act as the rudder that gently, and in alignment with the divine current, create our own unique and magnificently adorned journey in Soul Purpose.

This is the dynamic of Co-creation—letting go of "I, alone, make this happen"; recognizing the Divine Love, Wisdom, and Creativity present within and around us; setting intention; allowing grace to bring new possibilities forward; and using our authentically aligned choices and actions to manifest our Soul Purpose.

When we move from ego-creation to Co-creation and enlist the force that creates all form and possibility, we not only reside in the truth of our Soul Purpose faster and more consistently, but we also do so with more grace and ease. The result is more joy and love, far beyond what our ego originally envisioned as possible.

What is Co-creation?

We define Co-creation as the process by which you consciously partner with Spirit, universal wisdom, and creativity. Some people call this Divine Guidance or Grace. Joseph Campbell calls it Supernatural Aid. A sign you are in Co-creation is that you will experience flow, inspiration, joy, synchronicity, and unexpected surprises. Things just "magically" line up.

This partnership is in service to your growing awareness of who you truly are (everyone's Soul Purpose), as well as the manifestation of your goals and dreams in alignment with your highest good and the highest good of all concerned (the unique expression of your Soul Purpose).

To reside in love, and to live and serve from this state of loving, is what we are here on this planet to do. Loving is the highest good. So, it is through the act of connecting with your Higher Consciousness and partnering with Spirit that you receive the clarity and Divine Guidance for actions in alignment with your Soul Purpose and the highest good. This partnership is also one of freedom and expansiveness as you become both the recipient of and the conduit for the Source that created the universe.

Co-creation in Six Steps

How, then, do we move from ego-creation to Co-creation? This profound process is surprisingly simple in that it requires just six steps:

1. **Set a clear intention to connect with your True Self and receive guidance.** Sometimes, it is helpful to put your hand on your heart to connect more with that inner space of love and Higher Consciousness.

2. **Let go of attachment to preference or other blocks to receptivity.** Allow yourself to release any preconceptions about what guidance you will receive or the form it "should" take. Simply be open to what you experience right here and right now. If you are aware of mental or emotional blocks, such as limiting beliefs or judgments, bring acceptance and compassion to yourself so you can experience more peace and harmony.

3. **Attune, allow, and receive the inspiration and guidance that come forward.** Move into a space of inner stillness and quiet receptivity. Be open to any way

that the inspiration and guidance show up. It may be a picture that comes forward, or a message, a feeling, or a sense of something. Trust that this process supports you in "turning on the faucet," so however much or little you receive is fine. The faucet will continue to be on even after you complete this process.

4. **Lean into the guidance by taking action.** Once you receive guidance, consider what effective steps you could take to lean into that direction. (Note: You will be given additional guidance on how to create an effective action plan in later chapters of this book.) The process of leaning in or taking action in a particular direction is a highly effective way to test the validity of what you have received.

5. **Be present to any feedback from the action you have taken that indicates if you are on or off course.** As you lean into a direction through your actions, keep your eyes open. What feedback from the Universe are you receiving? Are you experiencing more "spiritual breadcrumbs" (a.k.a., innate joy, enthusiasm, aliveness, synchronicities, etc.)? Does the direction feel aligned? Feedback can come in many ways and many forms, so stay open and aware of what shows up for you.

6. **Refine your action plan by repeating steps 1–5.** Utilize the feedback you receive to make any refinements to your action plan. For example, you may have an inner hunch to contact a person, but you find that they are not the best source of expertise. However, that person suggests someone else, so you adjust your plan to make

a second contact. The path of Soul Purpose is a living thing that evolves and grows. Rather than thinking of it as a static plan, consider it as stepping-stones across a river. You discover each stone as you cross.

Engaging our Soul Purpose calls us into a greater level of the game. We can live in a much more expanded reality than our egos can conceive. We can learn to listen and partner with our True Self. When we connect with this level in our consciousness and allow the wisdom, inspiration, and synergy to flow through us, we can co-create beyond anything we could have conceived of or figured out. This approach *allows* it to happen as opposed to *making* it happen.

Most of us have direct experiences of this. However, we treat these experiences as random, rare, and lucky. But what if that quality of experience isn't a lucky happenstance but a way of being that we can learn how to avail ourselves of? What if experiencing those qualities is the very fabric of a life lived in true alignment with universal wisdom and creativity?

Preference Versus Soul Purpose

When we first venture into redirecting our lives toward purpose and impact, what frequently happens is that our minds latch onto a certain form that it "should" take in the world. In Mai Mai's story, it was her initial assumptions of the "best" way to navigate the river and what her experience "should" look like. In our daily lives, that "should" is influenced by what the ego deems important, such as status, money, safety, reputation, or conformity. Frequently in the Soul Purpose journey, that "should" takes the form of somehow "saving the world" or joining the "cause-du-jour."

This hybrid vision of purpose and ego is called "preference." That is, if we could have this venture go anywhere, this is what our preference would be. This is our choice right now for how we want it to show up.

On the surface, there is nothing wrong with having a preference. Through pure will and force, we may even bring our preference to life, regardless of whether it makes us more alive and fulfilled. There is even the chance that our preference is fully aligned with our Soul's plan for us.

But if we have set an intention to experience our Soul Purpose and truly be brought alive in this world, we may encounter a gap. The Source of Creation is the birthplace of infinite possibility and has infinitely greater awareness than our finite ego of the flatland. That Source may have something very different in form than we imagined. In order to truly fulfill our intention for living a more meaningful and joyful life, it may support us in experiencing the *essence* of what we are asking for, rather than the *form* (our preference), which we happen to be imagining at the time. Though perhaps unfamiliar to us, its approach offers an exponentially greater way to bring us alive, to connect us to our joy, and to provide us with deep and rich experiences of fulfillment beyond what we could have imagined.

When we move into collaboration with the Source that has created this entire universe—a universe that includes the beaming smiles of children, the alpine meadows in springtime, the grandeur of the Eagle Nebula, and the magic of a monarch butterfly emerging from a chrysalis—we are in for, at the very least, a slight pivot from our ego's preference.

When this type of gap occurs (and chances are good it will to some degree), we may find we keep hitting walls or closed doors as we force our will. If we are unaware of the difference between preference and purpose, we could spend fruitless hours trying to "make it happen." Just as Mai Mai's original struggles on the river illustrated, this type of egoic efforting often results in frustration and slow progress. Worse yet, we conclude from our lack of success that we are not one of the lucky ones that has a purpose or is good enough to fulfill it. If we remain attached to our preference and the form that it "must take," we may be inadvertently closing ourselves off from a much more expansive manifestation of our Soul Purpose.

However, when we are aware of both our preference and the deeper, truer, underlying purpose, we have greater freedom to open up to and move into alignment with Spirit and our True Self's calling. Similar to how the tumblers of a lock fall into place once the correct combination is found, when we move into this authentic alignment, there is grace, synchronicity, and flow. The results can appear to be magical and miraculous, but they are really signals that we are residing in and fulfilling our Soul Purpose.

There is an even more profound question and consideration: We could look at our Soul Purpose as not coming *from* us, but *through* us. In other words, what if the calling you are experiencing is one being made from Spirit through your Soul to you so that it can be manifested onto the planet at this time?

A Real-World Story: Doing Well and Doing Good

In what follows, Kirk describes an event during a particularly pivotal part of his Soul Purpose journey that demonstrates the power of moving from the limitedness of ego-creation and preference to the limitlessness of Co-creation:

Years before I understood my true Soul Purpose was to be a leadership coach, I was at the point where I knew I wanted my life to be purpose-oriented. Despite an odyssey of struggling, pushing, and trying to figure it out on the level of ego-creation, I could not make a connection between doing good and doing well with my work. I went right to my preferences: I tried to convince places I had worked for to start new divisions, tried to consult with businesses about purpose (back in 2006 before the idea was even well known), and even considered becoming a licensed marriage and family therapist. None of my preferences seemed to satisfy my need for purpose, for sustainment for my family, and to use my skills honed from years as a successful creative leader in the marketing world. There was a part of me that had started to deem it impossible and was pushing the rest of me to accept some kind of compromised default experience.

Around that time, I was watching a live interview between Oprah Winfrey and Eckhart Tolle. A woman called in and described in frustration how despite her best intentions she was not able to find her life calling, "I keep asking what I should do with my life, but I'm not getting any answer."

Of course, it felt familiar, so my ears perked up. This was exactly what had been going on in my own consciousness. Eckhart Tolle's response flipped the whole approach literally upside down: "If you find yourself asking it that way—'What should I do with my life?' and you are not getting an answer, then try asking it this way instead, 'Universe, what would You have me do with my life?'"

Immediately, I saw the brilliance and power in that. Inherent in the first version of the question was a request for an answer, formed from my preferences and not an invitation for Co-creation. In contrast, the second version of the question was an invitation for Co-creation: "What would You have me do with my life?"

In that precise moment, I changed my request to the Universe. I literally got down on my knees in my bedroom and, out loud, invited, "Universe, what would You have me do with my life?" And to be honest, I ask it that way again every day.

In a matter of a couple days, my phone rang. On the other end was a partner from a Washington, DC–based company I had never heard of (odd, as I'd been in the industry 20 years at that point), which, while an "ad agency," only did work for social causes (I did not know such a place could even exist) and was also the lead agency for Obama for America 2008 (something I had dreamed of being involved with but never thought remotely possible). The caller proceeded to offer me a position as Partner and Executive Creative Director at a salary that was quite comparable to what I had been receiving at a brand-oriented agency.

This was a scenario that my ego had already deemed impossible—purposeful, financially sustaining, and fully utilizing my creative skills. It was at a company that was a sizable force of 300 people doing great work in the world. It felt almost eerie to me at the time; in the move from ego-creation to Co-creation, suddenly a new world of possibility emerged. The opportunity before me couldn't have been more perfect if I had scripted it myself.

In a matter of weeks, my family and I had relocated to Washington, DC. My team and I had the opportunity to create scripts for the Obama campaign, to build a global pro-girl United Nations organization that we named and branded "Girl Up," and to bring to life a myriad of other causes that I had always dreamt of someday being able to serve. The apex of my experience was being able to work personally with then President Obama on his "Call to Service" campaign to invigorate Martin Luther King Jr. Day as a day of service. To shake hands with one of my true heroes, show him the creative off my laptop, including words for him to say, and then watch him deliver them on camera, was not a possibility I could have ever imagined for myself from my ego's view of possibility.

From an ego-creation perspective, I may have never arrived at this dream scenario. However, through inviting in Spirit as my partner—a benevolent force willing to create new possibilities for me to choose in tandem with my intentions and aligned actions—I was privileged to live in a vivid miraculous reality.

Co-creation in a Nutshell

Given their importance in your journey of Soul Purpose, the key takeaways from this chapter are summarized below in preparation for the activities that follow.

Co-creation is defined as a conscious partnering with Spirit, universal wisdom, and creativity. This partnership is in service to learning and growing in the awareness of who you truly are (everyone's Soul Purpose), as well as in manifesting your goals and dreams in alignment with your highest good and the highest good of all concerned (the unique expression of your Soul Purpose).

In contrast to the effort and struggle that often comes in ego-creation, the experience of conscious Co-creation can often be one of flow, ease, grace, and delightful synchronicities.

This is why it is important to distinguish between the ego's view of your vision and the deeper impulse that is your True Self calling. Preference is not necessarily Purpose. Preference is the out-picturing or form. It can show up as the ego's attachment to a particular definition of success—how it *should* look. Preference can be a form that comes from an attachment to a conditioned self-image because of "how I see myself or how I believe others see me. This is what I see my*self* doing." (Note: This is the small self, not the True Self.)

Purpose is the underlying impulse or essence from your True Self. Purpose is more foundational than form and, therefore, many forms can fulfill purpose.

Why does this matter? Because sometimes your preferences can be a more limited manifestation of the greater possibility available to you. If you are attached to manifesting your plan in the way that your current preferences dictate, you may be inadvertently closing yourself off to a much greater opportunity. When you are aware of both your preferences and your Purpose, you have greater freedom to open to what may be an exponentially bigger manifestation of your Purpose for yourself and for the planet—your true calling. The joy and fulfillment that come from connecting with your True Self and being used in greater service to yourself and to your world is where the magic happens.

Soul Purpose Practice

The following process was designed to support you in distinguishing between your ego's preferences and your Soul Purpose, and in freeing yourself from the confinement of the form and the restriction of being attached to a certain way your vision of impact "must" manifest. Additionally, it will assist you in moving into cooperation with the greater unfolding of your Soul Purpose and your unique opportunities for personal and professional impact.

You will be utilizing the first three steps of Co-creation as part of this process.

It is important to keep in mind that you are not committing to anything. You may come up with some ideas that may have no resonance for you, and you may discover others that really have energy. All are fine. The point is the creative exploration.

Clarifying and Connecting with Purpose

Set an intention to reside in connection with your True Self and the qualities of openness, creativity, and inspiration. See yourself as someone who is gifted, resourceful, and uniquely equipped to successfully fulfill the Soul Purpose that is being made manifest through you as you answer the following questions:

CLARIFYING PREFERENCE

1. What is your current vision of impact that you want to achieve? (Note: You may want to review the Soul Purpose Vision you created in Chapter 6.)

2. If this vision of impact were successful, what are your preferences as to what would be manifested?

CLARIFYING PURPOSE

3. What is your underlying motivation for manifesting this vision? What is the positive impact you want to make? In other words, what is your "why"?

4. Said another way, what is the opportunity for service that underlies your vision of impact? How are you being called to serve others? To serve your team? To contribute to the planet?

5. Given the distinction between your preference and the underlying service opportunity motivating you, do you see other ways that this deeper Soul Purpose could be fulfilled in your personal life? In your professional life? Share them. Remember, you are not committing to anything. This step is simply a way to open yourself to further creative exploration.

CONNECTING WITH PURPOSE

6. Move into a space of inner stillness, attunement, and quiet receptivity as you respond to the following questions:

    a. What is your sense of the essence of your True Self's calling or Soul Purpose? What is being brought through you to be manifested in the world at this time? (Note: This may be the same or a more expanded version of the Soul Purpose Vision you created in Chapter 6.)

    b. What wisdom, inspiration, or guidance does your True Self want to share?

7. Given all that you have explored and become aware of, take some time to update your Soul Purpose Vision.

8. Acknowledge yourself and your True Self for this time to come together in service to your Soul Purpose and unique contribution in the world.

9. Lastly, be aware of any feedback from the Universe that may appear from having done this process. Do not be surprised if you experience "spiritual breadcrumbs," such as innate joy, enthusiasm, synchronicities, etc.!

CHAPTER 8

OPENING TO
360° RECEPTIVITY

*"Every living thing is an engine geared to the wheelwork of
the Universe. Though seemingly affected only by its immediate
surroundings, the sphere of external influence extends to infinite
distance."*

—NIKOLA TESLA

M any years ago, a little girl named Suzanne Simard
became distressed when her beloved dog, Jigs, fell
into the hole of their family's outhouse and straight
down into the pool of what outhouses are meant to collect. Her
grandfather, a logger, got a shovel and began to dig in order to
retrieve poor Jigs from a scenario that most of us would not wish
on our worst enemies.

As a child in a family of loggers in the forests of British
Columbia, Suzanne had spent a lot of time in the forests, looking

upward at the majestic trees and marveling at their size and beauty. But now something new was being revealed to her. With each shovel full of soil being thrown up into the air, down in the ground a massive and intricate network of roots was being uncovered. The soil had been covering this vast other world from her, but now with its wondrous reality made visible, she was discovering the true bodies of forests. She would later become a distinguished professor of forest ecology at the University of British Columbia, and in 1997, that original moment of wonder as a girl, seeing the full truth of the forest, would lead to a remarkable discovery.

A Grand Interconnectedness

Professor Simard demonstrated to the world that trees talk to each other. Not only that, but trees also give of their own nutrients and immune defenses to other trees that need those things in order to keep them healthy and alive. Through vast underground networks called mycorrhizae, connected by the mycelial webs of fungi (mushrooms), trees listen to other trees in their stand, and often over vast distances, redistribute their nutrients to help other trees that are communicating need.

A sapling in the shade unable to generate for itself is given nutrients from other trees until it grows enough to reach the sun and be self-sufficient. What is even more remarkable, this underground conversation, generosity, and interdependence extended beyond species, with the cousins of firs and birches sharing with each other in need. In Professor Simard's words, they "were not in competition but in cooperation." Her research revealed that the forest was not so much a multitude of individual organisms, but one giant organism connected by a "sort of intelligence."

While this discovery is truly awe-inducing and even magical, from our perspective it also makes logical and empirical sense.

Let's start with the birth of our physical universe. Whether our context is science or spirituality, inflation theory or creation theory, it seems there is a basic agreement that everything sprang from one thing. Choose your own context and concept for what that one thing is—a singularity, God, Source, energy, consciousness, etc.—all will work perfectly in terms of the postulate put forward here.

If everything sprang from one thing, that one thing must be *in* everything. Everything that exists must simply be a different expression or permutation of that one thing. Every form, every question, every answer. Everything you can think, everything you can see, everything you can experience. Every star, every mustard seed, every human, every fir, and every birch. They must all be, in some manner or structure, comprised of that one thing.

If that is accurate, then this essence is throughout all things and all things are connected by it. Like the massive mycorrhiza network Suzanne obliviously walked on every day, this connection may not always be visible to us and yet it is the very foundation connecting everything we see. Suzanne's gaze began upward and therefore all the trees appeared as individual beings, but when circumstances took her awareness downward to the network below, that illusion of separate tree-beings dissolved into the thick forest air. Similarly, as we walk our world and see the myriad of life-forms all around us, might we also be mistakenly seeing separate beings when, in fact, we are only perceiving the equivalent of the trees above the ground? Might there be a level, beyond which we can currently see, where we are not in competition with each other, but in constant connection and cooperation?

As Professor Simard summed up, "The forest is more than you can see."

It would stand to reason, then, that when one of those myriad of forms or beings would have a need or intention, just like a sapling in the shade, that this would be communicated through an even more pervasive, powerful, cosmic mycorrhiza made of the one thing that became all things. And therefore, all things around us would, at that moment, be prompted to provide us with the information, ideas, knowing, and inspiration to fulfill that need or intention.

The only thing that then determines if that transaction is complete is our ability to receive it. Is our outstretched hand open or closed? Are we able to open our awareness beyond what we may currently be able to perceive so that as the world around us responds and shares with us—whether that's through another person, a raindrop, a dream, a cherry pie, an early morning inspiration, or an unexpected detour on the way home—we will be open enough to recognize it for what it is?

We call this 360° Receptivity. It is available to all of us because it is a manifestation of our very nature: a forest of forms that are seemingly separate, yet simultaneously comprise one miraculous singular organism connected by an intelligence conspiring to have us all succeed and thrive.

The Guidance All Around Us

We believe each person receives constant direction and guidance. Our Soul or True Self—that part of us intrinsically connected to the greater Love, Wisdom, and Creativity of the Divine—is continually in conversation with that great Source, partnering with It to provide us support and clues in our Soul Purpose journey. But most of us are so caught up in the flatland of our ego's limited perspective that, metaphorically, we do not lift our eyes to see what is all around us.

To benefit from this unlimited support requires keeping our eyes open and being willing to receive the guidance available. This is 360° Receptivity. It is based upon an active awareness that we are in co-creation and collaboration with *all* that is around us: people, situations, environments, and events that make up our physical reality, as well as the inner promptings, dreams, synchronicities, and grace that make up our greater reality.

There are many great examples of the power of 360° Receptivity. Have you ever heard of Bill Klan? If you are like most you have not, nor had we. This unknown colleague of Henry Ford was the inspiration behind modern manufacturing. One day, Klan shared with Ford a process he had observed in which butchers quickly worked together to create various cuts of meat. This same approach in reverse would become Ford's assembly line.

360° Receptivity means we are aware that Divine Support, Wisdom, and Creativity can flow to us through *anything*, including, as in the case of Ford, a passing comment by a colleague.

Musician Paul McCartney received the melody of the song "Yesterday" during a dream. When he woke up, he immediately went to the piano so he would not lose the song in his awakened state. Dreams, commutes, and showers are familiar playgrounds for 360° Receptivity.

Peter Diamandis and Steven Kotler in their book *Bold* encourage the reader to "look for ideas everywhere." Wisdom, inspiration, and guidance can come at any time, in any form. The more we are open, the more opportunity we have of receiving.

There is a constant flow of wisdom, insights, answers, beauty, and magic swirling all around us. One of the most fundamental and productive exercises we can give our consciousness in service to our Soul Purpose is to constantly push and stretch our aperture of perception and possibility.

Creating Magic Through Receptivity

In his book *Creating Magic: 10 Common Sense Leadership Strategies from a Life at Disney*, Lee Cockerell relays an experience when he was an Executive Vice President of Operations for the Disney organization that was pivotal to his own leadership philosophy and illustrates the power of 360° Receptivity. At the time, the Disney hotel bookings were dropping mysteriously. None of the executives in charge of hospitality had any idea why.

One day, Lee was in one of the Disney Park hotels. His policy was to connect with any employee, no matter their position, so he struck up a conversation with one of the housekeeping staff. He shared about the drop in room occupation, and she responded by telling him it was because they no longer gave the beautiful gifts they used to. The gift packages that greeted hotel guests were relatively inexpensive, so logically it seemed as if this would not be the reason; however, Lee leaned into the housekeeper's advice, reinstituted the welcome gifts for hotel guests, and the room occupation rates returned to their regular high levels.

Had Lee not been open to feedback coming from an unusual source, he and his team might never have resolved their problem. If he had deemed himself "too busy" or "too important" to take the time to talk with one of his employees, he would have inadvertently blocked himself from the universal guidance available to him at that moment.

Fortunately for him and the hospitality team, he did not. Yet how easy it is for us to rush through our days, missing what may be many attempts by the Universe to support us.

Opening to 360° Receptivity

In the last chapter, we shared one of our favorite metaphors for the Soul Purpose journey—crossing the river one stepping-stone at a time. The ego yearns to be given the location of all the stepping-stones (with easy-to-follow instructions!) before it makes the crossing. However, that next stone is often only revealed just after we have stepped precariously onto the last one.

Steve Jobs said it this way: "You can't connect the dots looking forward; you can only connect them looking backwards. So you have to trust that the dots will somehow connect in your future. You have to trust in something—your gut, destiny, life, karma, whatever."

Why would that be? If we were still running a Story of Limitation, we might get frustrated and point to this as evidence of how tough life is. However, we are well past that trap. Seeing through the eyes of the True Self, it becomes evident that this dynamic supports us in being more present with ourselves, others, the environment, and the journey itself.

Life happens in the present moment. Grace happens when we are present to it.

As the river metaphor indicates, Soul Purpose is a journey into the unknown, or what we like to call the Field of Infinite Potential. This journey takes courage and a willingness to be open and vulnerable, and to cooperate with a plan greater than us (and at times, beyond our current awareness).

This strength of heart, openness, willingness, and devotion are all qualities of the True Self. If our ultimate Soul Purpose is to awaken more fully into our awareness of who we truly are, then it makes complete sense that the design of this Universe and our journey would continually encourage us to reside more in these qualities. Universal design supports us in climbing up the butte, not staying in the flatlands. It encourages us to open to our inner guidance, synchronicities, chance encounters, sudden inspiration, and other spiritual breadcrumbs.

Following the Spiritual Breadcrumbs

Do you recall the fairytale of Hansel and Gretel? In the story, two children are lost in the woods and use breadcrumbs as means to try to make their way back home. The popularity of breadcrumbs in this fairytale inspired the use of the same word to mean the navigational device used in software programs and documents. Similarly, there are spiritual breadcrumbs that we can follow in our journey of Soul Purpose. In addition to the dreams, sudden inspiration, chance encounters, and other synchronicities mentioned above, spiritual breadcrumbs can also take the form of enthusiasm, joy, aliveness, synchronicity, and loving service. These are qualities of the True Self. When they are present, it is most often a sign from our Higher Consciousness and the Universe that we are on course as we journey home to who we truly are.

A Real-World Story: Music for the Heart

Eoghan had a deep love of music, particularly dance music, and he felt his greatest connection to himself and others when he was deejaying. Eoghan had joined a weekly gathering that Kirk hosts called "Rumi's Field," where people get together in a loving and compassionate space to discuss the challenges in their lives and address them together through many of the principles in this book.

Eoghan is the father of a wonderful little girl, whom he loves with all his heart. With that love came a great sense of responsibility for Eoghan—a responsibility that many of us are familiar with: the one that says perhaps it's time to put away the dream and instead save for the things little girls need, like books, shoes, and food. It's a reasonable responsibility and Eoghan took it seriously. He took jobs that sometimes related to music (working in commercial audio houses doing the work of preparing and archiving sessions, etc.) and sometimes didn't.

Eoghan was resigned to the belief that what he perceived as his true dream—to be a DJ bringing joy to thousands of people by performing and making dance tracks—was not in the cards for him. Of the thousands of DJs in the world, only a micro-percentage get the kind of remuneration that allows them to support themselves, and only a micro-percentage of those make enough to support a family. Simply doing something that was even *related* to music (i.e., the commercial music houses) was the highest aspiration he dared to embrace.

But in a moment of suspending that Story of Limitation and opening up to 360° Receptivity, Eoghan looked out at his surrounding audiences for what was the bigger purpose under his dream of deejaying. In their joyous faces and bouncing bodies, all connected by his music like the mycorrhiza of the trees, came the feedback he needed. He saw that what made him come alive was the joy, bliss, and healing he witnessed by connecting people to their own Souls through music. This awareness enabled Eoghan to look differently at what his Soul Purpose intention might be. He chose to open the aperture a bit and see that while deejaying may be one way of connecting people to their innate Souls and joy through music, there was no proof that it was the *only* way. As he opened his hand around his intention, as opposed to keeping it tightly closed around his DJ preference, his intention blossomed into *serving others by connecting them to their authentic selves through music.*

But the work wasn't done. Next came the letting go of many of his myths that created inaction, such as self-judgments about his self-worth, his deserving joy, the importance of others' opinions of him, etc.

By facing those self-judgments and releasing them, Eoghan gave himself permission to take action and put himself out there to activate even more 360° Receptivity. Eoghan began to openly share his new intention and reach out to anyone and any opportunity that seemed even remotely close to its realization. Those actions unshackled his Universe and providence toward Co-creation. Eoghan heard from a friend in an organization helping inner-city kids in juvenile detention centers use music to heal their feelings and trauma. One of the ways the organization did this was through the creation of rhythms and backdrop beats to inspire them to write rhymes about their stories and feelings. The organization was looking to fill a position with someone who knew how to create those kinds of beats. Eoghan had a lot of fear and trepidation. His self-judgments around his worthiness, imposter syndrome around his own background of "white privilege," etc. reared their ugly heads, but Eoghan stayed on the ride despite the fear.

Eoghan put his hat in the ring and got the position. He worked in juvenile detention centers, mixed beats for the kids, heard their rhymes about their lives, and saw them open up for perhaps the very first time. Suddenly, Eoghan saw something miraculous: He was using his musical gifts, particularly the creation of dance beats, to connect people—and not just any people, but people with deep and real need—to their Souls and authentic selves. He was living a scenario he had never even imagined was out there—a scenario where he was truly healing people through music that was made possible by letting go of his original preference and opening to the Universe.

And it didn't end there.

One day, while in the detention center, there was a new batch of kids, and no one was taking the step forward to share. Something then moved through Eoghan—an action in such alignment with his intention that despite it going against his deepest fears, he chose to do anyway. Eoghan opened up to the group about his own feelings—his judgments and guilt about his relatively safe upbringing in an Irish suburb, his self-judgments around white privilege, his sense of unworthiness to be making this kind of music without what some might say are the required authentic cultural roots, etc. His voice was shaky being this vulnerable in front of such a battle-hardened group, but it was that vulnerability and uncommon receptivity to the kids around him that opened things up and allowed the kids to begin to come forward themselves. At the end of the session, many came up to Eoghan to bump fists, pat him on the back, and even give hugs of reassurance and gratitude that he was there.

Eoghan then had an epiphany that his intention of helping people connect with their Souls and authenticity through music *had always included himself.* And the Universe, together with the kids, had just given him that gift.

Soul Purpose Practice

Assessing and Enhancing Your 360° Receptivity

The following self-discovery questions and activity are designed to support you in opening to 360° Receptivity so that you can more fully collaborate with and benefit from Universal Guidance, regardless of the form it takes.

Set an intention for honesty, openness, engaged exploration, and receptivity as you answer the following questions.

Assessing Your Current Process of Receiving Feedback

This first set of questions will assist you in clarifying how effectively you receive both positive feedback (e.g., compliments and acknowledgements) and negative or course-corrective feedback. As you explore this aspect of receptivity, it is helpful to keep in mind that feedback from others is comprised of two parts: 1) the information attempting to be relayed and 2) the energy it rides on.

- When someone authentically acknowledges or compliments you, do you find yourself dismissing it? How fully do you receive a compliment? How fully do you receive the positive energy that it rides on? On a scale of 1 to 9 (with 1 being "hardly at all" and 9 being "very"), rate your effectiveness in receiving this type of feedback from the Universe:

    1   2   3   4   5   6   7   8   9

- When someone provides you with negative or course-corrective feedback, do you find that you defend yourself? (Hint: You may even find that this question stirs up a little defensiveness. If it does, that's feedback!) To what degree do you receive the information, regardless of the energy that it is riding on? Rate your effectiveness in receiving this type of feedback from the Universe:

  1   2   3   4   5   6   7   8   9

Assessing Your 360° Receptivity

This next set of questions will support you in clarifying how receptive you are to the feedback coming from your physical environment, such as other people or situations you encounter in your daily life, as well as how receptive you are to serendipity—that type of synchronistic or "magical" feedback coming from the Universe.

- How open are you in receiving feedback from people you deem authority figures? Rate your effectiveness in receiving this type of feedback from the Universe:

  1   2   3   4   5   6   7   8   9

- How open are you in receiving feedback from people to whom you are a teacher, mentor, supervisor, or caregiver?

Rate your effectiveness in receiving this type of feedback from the Universe:

1   2   3   4   5   6   7   8   9

- How open are you to receiving feedback from people you deem your colleagues (i.e., friends, siblings, team members, and coworkers)? Rate your effectiveness in receiving this type of feedback from the Universe:

1   2   3   4   5   6   7   8   9

- How open are you to receiving feedback from situations or the environment? For example, learning from other's experiences, educational offerings, events you read in the news and see on TV, and situations you encounter. Rate your effectiveness in receiving this type of feedback from the Universe:

1   2   3   4   5   6   7   8   9

- How receptive are you to feedback that comes in the form of "coincidence" or synchronicity? For example, you want to get a certain form of assistance, and the next day you get a call from someone who could provide that type of support, or you run across an article or ad that provides a lead. Rate your effectiveness in receiving this type of feedback from the Universe:

1   2   3   4   5   6   7   8   9

- How open are you to receiving feedback from your dreams, from inspiration in the shower, or from when you are taking a walk or driving? Rate your effectiveness in receiving this type of feedback from the Universe:

  1   2   3   4   5   6   7   8   9

- How open are you to receiving feedback during meditation, contemplation, chanting, or prayer—whichever way that you consciously connect with your Higher Self and the Universe or Spirit? Rate your effectiveness in receiving this type of feedback from the Universe:

  1   2   3   4   5   6   7   8   9

- How open are you to receiving feedback from other spiritual breadcrumbs—experiences of enthusiasm, joy, aliveness, and loving service? Rate your effectiveness in receiving this type of feedback from the Universe:

  1   2   3   4   5   6   7   8   9

Enhancing Your 360° Receptivity

This final activity can support you in utilizing what you have learned in service to opening more fully to the feedback that is available to you.

- Review the ten rating scales above. Consider which of the areas of feedback you want to enhance.

- Select one or two areas of feedback that you are willing to experiment with in the next 30 days.

- Set an intention for the next 30 days to be open to and aware of opportunities for enhancing the area(s). (Note: The reason we suggest a period of 30 days is that we have found most egos are open to trying an experiment but reluctant to commit to anything for a long period of time. A length of one month works well for most people, but feel free to adjust this length to one that works best for you.)

- Keep a daily journal in which you note the opportunities for enhanced feedback and what you did to enhance your effectiveness and receptivity.

- If you find yourself challenged by your experiment, not to worry. That in and of itself is feedback! The very fact that you are more aware of it means you are making progress. The beauty of conducting this experiment is that you can make adjustments to enhance your effectiveness.

- Acknowledge yourself daily during this 30-day experiment to provide positive feedback to yourself and to support your ongoing commitment to your learning and growth.

CHAPTER 9

TURNING DOWNTIME INTO DOWNLOAD TIME

"Stillness is where creativity and solutions to problems are found."

—ECKHART TOLLE

I magine inside of us is a great conduit.

Let's call it the conduit of creation.

It is the passageway through which the new and miraculous come through us into our world.

As with any conduit in our universe, the flow moves in one direction at a time. Like the tides we witness as we stand on the beach, the flow in this conduit moves in or out. Up or down. This way or that way.

Now imagine on one end of the conduit of creation is our mind, our mental and thinking self, the self that likes to devour information, file things away, strategize, lead operations, and in general, be busy either absorbing or doing things. The mind is the aspect of us that takes the grand blueprints of the architect, finds the pertinent information, and diligently develops and executes a construction plan.

Then imagine on the other end of the conduit is our essence, our heart, our True Self that is always connected to the fountainhead of Divine Creativity that generated our entire universe and perhaps many, many others. It generated every form, every star, every seed, every being, every thought, every giggle of a child, every call of the starling, every question, every answer, every color, every celestial event, every dewdrop, every particle, and every wave; everything you can imagine and everything you can't. For those of you more science-minded, one could also describe what lies at this end as what physicist Paul Dirac first called the "quantum field"—that place of pure formless infinite possibility from which all things come into emergence.

The flow from the end of the mind—the absorber, filer, thinker—is from out to in. The mind is focused on those things that already exist. In contrast, the flow from our True Self is from in to out. The intention is to birth into reality those things that have never existed before.

Aligning to the Flow from the Source

When we want to be generative, to be visionary, to do more than replicate or simply add a new flavor to the old; when the moment arrives to transcend what *is*, to bring forth what *will be*; when the moment arrives to be the midwife to the birth of something truly evolutionary to us and perhaps to our world—from where do we want the flow to be coming? From the mind, or from the Source of Creation?

Our recommendation, if we are wanting to fully imagine and envision how our Soul Purpose is going to be co-created in this world, is that we align ourselves to the flow that comes from the Source.

This means the direction of the flow is from our essence, heart, True Self, rather than from the other direction. While the mind may have been very busy serving us well by absorbing, filing, doing, thinking, and constructing, if we want the kind of innovative ideas, insights, and visions that are beyond the mind, we will need to cease that activity, allowing the flow to reverse. Then, the direction comes from a place of infinite possibility inside us, outward, toward and through the mind to be expressed in the world.

It is perhaps one of the most life-changing revelations we can have—that the greatest level of creation available to us lies not in the busyness, but in the silence.

Not in the movement, but in the stillness.

Not in the making, but in the allowing.

Not in the mind, but in the heart.

Opening to Inspiration and Guidance

Now that you are becoming more aware of the True Self, it is important to develop ways to connect with this fountainhead of guidance, wisdom, inspiration, and creativity. A highly effective way of receiving inspiration and guidance is by making time to be still and receptive. We included Eckhart Tolle's quotation at the beginning of this chapter because it is even more relevant given the time in which we live. The world is urging us to be more productive—jump online more, check your phone more, do more, and do it faster. However, the latest science indicates this is a great untruth.

According to engineering professor Barbara Oakley, author of *A Mind for Numbers: How to Excel at Math and Science (Even If You Flunked Algebra)*, in addition to this "focused mode," which relies on the brain's prefrontal cortex, we also learn through a "diffuse mode," rooted in the operations of a variety of different brain regions. In fact, the brain switches back and forth between these modes regularly. Oakley explains, "When you're focusing, you're actually blocking your access to the diffuse mode. And the diffuse mode, it turns out, is what you often need to be able to solve a very difficult, new problem." Or, going back to our metaphor of a conduit, "focused mode" creates an inward flow from the mind and prohibits an outward flow of true creativity and innovation that emerges from the deeper source of Divine Creation.

David Burkus of *Harvard Business Review* explains exactly why breaks lead to creative breakthroughs: The researchers found that the group given a break to work on an unrelated task generated the most ideas....One possible explanation for these findings is that...when you work on a problem continuously, you can become fixated on previous solutions....Taking a break from the problem and focusing on something else entirely gives the mind some time to release its fixation on the same solutions and let the old pathways fade from memory. Then, when you return to the original problem, your mind is more open to new possibilities—eureka moments.

It was simply by contemplating a sunset that Nikola Tesla had the insight about rotating magnetic fields, which in turn led to the development of the modern day alternating current electrical mechanism.

From a Soul Purpose context, it is important to create the opportunity to leave the thinking mind, move into the stillness, and thereby access the deeper creativity of the True Self where new and game-changing ideas and inspiration occur.

In other words:

Leave your mind open to the deeper creativity of your True Self.

Author William Keiper says it this way:

In order to access and create that energy, we need to do some things we may not have done for a long time. Go outside and breathe the air, sit on a boulder in the sun, lie in the grass, listen to the wind in the trees. Take the time to look at the stars and the clouds, to sit outside for an hour in the middle of the night, to listen to the quiet offered by a new blanket of snow. All of these things and more can provide needed space for your creative mind to generate and engage the energy for creating the rest of your life.

How many times have you experienced this? When you are out in nature, or taking a shower, or doing something other than concentrating, suddenly the inspiration comes. That is why we encourage practices that support inner stillness and receptivity, such as meditation and being out in nature. These are ways to support yourself in slowing down and connecting with the wisdom and inspiration that is your essential nature.

As you do, you leave the ego's paradigm and injunction of "I have to figure it out" and enter the paradigm of the True Self—an inner sanctuary of stillness, non-doing, allowing, and receptivity.

A Real-World Story: Lying Down on the Job

The following story illustrates a few important keys in the Soul Purpose journey: 1) the power of downtime as a way into greater connection and creativity, 2) how easy it is to forget to prioritize these times of stillness in the busyness of daily life, and 3) how despite that forgetfulness, our True Self in cooperation with the Universe will conspire to support us in creating these times of quietude.

Licia recounts her story:

I was in the midst of a very intense period of productivity. At the time, Kirk and I were developing our first Soul Purpose workshop, and we were both enrolled in a 10-month Soul-Centered Professional Coaching Program. Additionally, I had my full-time university job as the Managing Director of Programs, Admissions, and Marketing, was teaching one weekend per month, and had my own private coaching practice—definitely a busy and very demanding time!

It was also a highly creative time, both in my co-design of Soul Purpose with Kirk and my design of new approaches for programs and digital marketing for the university. Innovation and creativity have always been the most exciting activities for me, so I happily ignored the signs that I was overextending myself. I was bypassing my own inner guidance to create times of rest, respite, and rejuvenation.

One morning as I was packing up for a day at the university, my back went out. I literally could not stand up. I ended up on the floor, flat on my back, in our guest bedroom. Fortunately, my husband was home, and inch by painful inch he was able to help me get in the bed of the guest room. At that point, I wasn't even able to move a few feet down the hall to our bedroom.

I ended up in that bed for three full days. Given my constitution and consuming work schedule, this unexpected three-day sojourn was unheard of for me. From my ego's perspective, it was at the worst possible time with major deadlines bearing down on me. I was in the midst of a highly demanding launch campaign, which required my creative direction and supervision.

Yet here I was unable to move, to go to work, to even get onto my laptop.

All I had was time and me.

And that's when an amazing thing happened.

The director of marketing, who was my direct report at the time and whom I hadn't yet alerted of my back issue, reached out for my support with a key aspect of a new campaign. She was in the midst of developing a recommendation for the campaign's main messaging and positioning, which was due that day. I could hear the concern and urgency in her voice. Had I been up and about, I might have joined her there. But I had been stationary for a couple hours before she called, so I was already in a calm, still place. Rather than telling her I was out on a sick day, I heard a quiet inner voice instructing me to simply sit with her request, so I asked her to give me some time and I would call her back.

Then, I did just that, not sit but lay there with her request. I didn't feel pressured to save the day by coming up with ideas. I just felt open to possibility that ideas would come. Mostly, I felt serene, still, and receptive.

And the ideas did come. Multiple variations of approaches we could take presented themselves to me. Some of them seemed okay, others quite exciting, but all of them were new solutions to the existing request.

Had I attempted to "figure out" an answer, I would have been looking for what had worked well in the past, or what seemed best to implement given the timeframe; however, both of these approaches would have been mental suggestions from my ego. Because I was forced to be still, I found myself in an inner quiet space, free of distractions and busyness where I could receive a wealth of fresh, innovative approaches.

In those three days, I entered a co-creative playground with my True Self and Spirit. By slowing down, getting still, and setting intentions, I was able to receive wisdom and inspiration on a variety of topics and projects. The key was to remain open and quietly receptive.

Not only did this support the marketing director's timely delivery, but it also supported me in having a clear, direct, and extended experience of the power of downtime—synchronistically, during the very time I was developing the educational content and processes for Soul Purpose. Coincidence? I think not.

Soul Purpose Practice

Tracking True-Self Guidance

We have all experienced those delightful moments when we receive unexpected inspiration. The opportunity is to become more familiar with those moments when they occur, including where we are in consciousness when they do.

This brief process will support you in reflecting upon the times you have received inspiration and guidance. Set an intention to reside in the qualities of inner stillness, openness, and receptivity as you answer the following questions.

1. Consider the last week or month. Are you aware of any times that you experienced unexpected inspiration or guidance? If you do not remember any recent times, reflect on any times in the past when inspiration or guidance has unexpectedly shown up.

2. Describe those times. What was happening? When and how did you receive the inspiration or guidance?

3. What were (or weren't) you doing during those times? Was it during a time that you were focused on finding a solution, or was it during a time when your focus was elsewhere, such as taking a shower, going on a run, meditating, praying, driving, socializing, etc.?

4. In general, how do you respond when you receive these gifts of guidance? Do you respond with acknowledgment and gratitude? Do you take time to write down the inspiration? Or do you take these moments for granted?

5. Are there ways for you to create more inner receptivity in service to living more fully in your Soul Purpose? This may be through creating more Downtime/Download (D2) time in your schedule, or it may simply be that you more fully acknowledge and honor the inspiration when it comes. What would work best for you? Describe it here.

6. Are you willing to commit to any of your ideas? If yes, we encourage you to conduct an experiment and commit to trying one or more of your ideas over the next 30 days. Write down which one(s) you are willing to experiment with during that time.

7. Acknowledge yourself for your True Self support!

One final note: Once you complete your 30-day experiment (or whatever length of time you committed to), you may want to recommit to another round of experimenting with D2 times.

Bonus Round: Experimenting with D2 Times

If you identified ways that you could move into a more receptive, co-creative space in the practice above, we encourage you to use the process below as a way to gain the most from your D2 times. Set an intention for residing in the wisdom and clarity of your True Self and answer the following questions immediately after you complete each of your D2 times.

1. What did you experience during this process? What qualities of your True Self did you connect to?

2. What inspiration or guidance did you receive?

3. What benefit(s) did you receive through your participation? How does this support your efforts to live more fully in your True Self and/or Soul Purpose?

4. In what ways could you enhance your D2 times?

5. Acknowledge yourself and your True Self for taking the time to connect in support of your Soul Purpose.

CHAPTER 10

CREATING YOUR SOUL PURPOSE PLAN

"The moment one definitely commits oneself, then providence moves, too. All sorts of things occur to help one that would never otherwise have occurred. A whole stream of events issue from the decision, raising in one's favor all manner of unforeseen incidents, meetings, and material assistance, which no man could have dreamed would have come his way. Whatever you can do or dream you can, begin it. Boldness has genius, power and magic in it. Begin it now."

—WILLIAM HUTCHISON MURRAY

Imagine you are surrounded by a loving, creative intelligence that is just waiting to support you in co-creating your Soul Purpose and bring forward opportunities, people, and events to support your journey and awaken you to your True Self.

How do you best partner with this benevolent Source? Throughout this book, you have been introduced to the Soul Purpose Method, which offers a three-phase approach with practices designed to work in harmony with your True Self and Spirit. The final step of this approach is to develop and commit to a Soul Purpose Action Plan. This plan is created from your Northstar Intention and Soul Purpose Vision. It is refined by your review and integration of the 360° feedback you receive.

Your Northstar Intention

Throughout this book, you have had opportunities to set different intentions. You will notice that many activities started with a suggestion to set an intention. We both utilize this practice of intention setting multiple times throughout our day: at the beginning of meetings or writing sessions, at the start of coaching sessions, and before we drive, to name a few. The process of aligning ourselves with what we want to be experiencing, as well as asking for assistance from Spirit, supports us in more consistently residing in the consciousness of our True Selves. It is a way to return to our inner center again and again as we navigate our lives.

Additionally, you have had the opportunity to create a Northstar Intention. As a reminder, this intention will evolve depending on where you are in your journey of Soul Purpose. The key is for the intention to be positive, genuine, in your own words, and uplifting for you. Your intention should "speak to you," meaning you should feel enthused when you say it. Once you have created your clear, positive Northstar Intention, we encourage you to say it often. Post it on your refrigerator, at your bedside, and as your screensaver on your computer or mobile devices. Doing so will support you in keeping it fresh in your awareness.

Your Soul Purpose Vision

Once you have created your Northstar Intention, the next step is to expand it into a Soul Purpose Vision. This is a detailed description of you living your Soul Purpose. It answers the question: If I were currently living my Soul Purpose, what would I be experiencing? What would I be doing or feeling? How would I be interacting with others and myself? In what ways would I be serving?

At the end of this chapter, you will have the opportunity to refine the vision that you have developed in the practices from earlier chapters.

Creating Your Soul Purpose Action Plan

After you have created your Soul Purpose Vision, you develop actions in alignment with this vision. We have found that people often are challenged with this step simply because they are not clear on how to create action steps that are easy to commit to and complete.

Five Criteria for Creating Effective Action Steps

When you are designing an action step, ensure that it is

1. **Specific and trackable.** Steps should be clear and detailed, rather than vague. It should be easy to know when you have completed the action. For example, the action, "I'm going to reach out to friends to see what community service projects I'd like to get involved in" is not trackable because it does not have the specificity to determine when it is complete. It does not include the number of friends, the specific friends, or the timeframe within which the action should be completed. A more effective version could be: "I will call Melinda and Francisco by the end of the week and ask them if they know of any local service projects. I'll leave a voice message if I don't reach them." See how it will be easy to know when this action step is completed?

2. **Doable by you—within your own power to complete.** It is easy to create an action step that is dependent on another's action; however, this makes the completion of that step something that is out of your control. For example, "I'm going to get the lead in a Broadway musical" is an ineffective action step because its completion is dependent on the director or producer hiring you for the part. Instead, "I'm going to audition for the musical" keeps the action doable and not contingent upon anyone else.

3. **Designed keeping in mind "floors not ceilings."** In your enthusiasm to make progress on your Soul

Purpose, it can be a temptation to overcommit. When developing ongoing action steps that support new, positive habits or routines, the adage "less is more" applies. For example, "I'm going to start my new daily meditation practice by sitting for two hours each day" is an action that most people will find quite difficult to sustain. Consider the minimal commitment that will support your progress (the "floor") rather than a big stretch (the "ceiling"). In the same example, if you were just starting to meditate, a five-minute or ten-minute daily commitment would be a great way to build this new habit.

4. **Parsed as micro-commitments.** This is similar to criteria #3 but applies to all action steps, whether or not they are ongoing. Ensure that your action steps are small and easily achievable. Let's say you want to be of service by donating money from the proceeds of a garage sale to a local food bank. A small, achievable action step might be to "clear one closet of old clothes" or "make signs for the sale," rather than setting an action step of "having a garage sale." The latter is a project requiring many steps, rather than a single action step. International coach and author Steve Chandler in his book *Crazy Good* explains how essential small steps are for success: "That desire to make some quantum Knievel jump across the canyon from failure to success. And then being scared to do it. And then, eventually, trying the big leap and failing. All the while not understanding that transformation can occur beautifully with tiny, tiny steps."

5. **Represents the next step in front of you right now.**
   When embarking on what may be a grand new vision of Soul Purpose, it can be easy to feel overwhelmed by all that you sense you must do. One antidote to overwhelm is simply focusing on the very next step in front of you. In most cases, it is easy to identify that next step. You do not need to pressure yourself to figure out the entire plan. From our experience, that is not how co-creation works. As we have said before, the process is more akin to crossing a river, where the next stepping-stone appears when you need it.

Committing to Action

Once you do clarify an action step and commit to it, it is very important to keep your agreement with yourself. This builds self-trust, which is foundational to success. If you become aware that you will not be able to complete an action that you have committed to, it is equally important to renegotiate that commitment with yourself and with others, if applicable. This means that you evaluate what you can do when you are able to complete it, and recommit to the new approach and timing. Renegotiation will preserve the integrity of your commitment, which is essential for maintaining a healthy relationship with yourself and others.

Receiving Feedback and Refining Your Plan

Do you recall the six steps for Co-creation? They are:

1. Set a clear intention to connect with your True Self and receive guidance.

2. Let go of attachment to preference or other blocks to receptivity.

3. Attune, allow, and receive the inspiration and guidance that come forward.

4. Lean into the guidance by taking action.

5. Be present to any feedback from the action you have taken that indicates if you are on or off course.

6. Refine your action plan by repeating steps 1 through 5.

As you engage in this six-step process, stay present and vigilant to any feedback (positive or negative) that you are receiving. This is where your awareness and practice of 360° Receptivity comes into play. Part of engaging with 360° Receptivity involves remembering that any type of feedback can be useful. Positive feedback can often signal that we are on track in our direction. Negative feedback is just as useful, as it signals potential opportunities for adjustments to our plan. It can signal, just as it did with Serene and her burgeoning nonprofit for social impact, that the Universe is attempting to support the fulfillment of our Soul Purpose Vision in new and unexpected ways. Or it can be a sign, just as it did for Kirk, that his vision of providing greater service was limited and had the opportunity to expand into breathtaking new possibilities. That is why we prefer to use the more accurate term "course-corrective feedback" because there is no negative feedback if we utilize it effectively.

Residing in Gratitude for Yourself and Your Journey

Lastly, it is important to reside in gratitude for yourself. It is no small thing to live a life in alignment with your Soul Purpose. It requires that you bravely step out of your comfort zone and into new inner and outer terrain. This lifelong journey takes courage and strength of heart. We encourage you—do not mistake loving self-acknowledgment for conceit. As author Rick Warren says in *The Purpose Driven Life*: "Humility is not thinking less of yourself, it's thinking of yourself less."

False humility is the game of the ego. When we acknowledge and thank ourselves, we are positively reinforcing our own new behaviors and actions, and we will tend then to repeat them more. This is the most sacred work—to follow your Soul's calling and live the life waiting for you.

Gratitude is a quality of the True Self. Residing in gratitude for yourself and your life supports you in connecting with your authentic nature, which recognizes the beauty of this sacred journey of learning, loving, and growth.

Lastly, it is important to reside in gratitude for the support that you are receiving and the support you may yet receive—no matter if that support comes in ways you had hoped or if it shows up in new and different ways. It is important in terms of our inner well-being and enjoying more of the outer experiences we want. Recent research from Robert A. Emmons, Ph.D., at the University of California, Davis, shows that people who practice gratitude experience 25 percent higher happiness, and that the experience of gratitude literally changes the neural pathways and has people move into action that, in turn, creates more experiences for which to be grateful.

In our relationship with Spirit and the Universe, when we practice gratitude, we naturally create a state of receptivity that opens us to more positive experiences, which is often responded to by the Universe in kind. As Meister Eckhart, theologian, said: "If the only prayer you said was thank you, that would be enough."

A Real-World Story: A Fresh Prince

Long before we encountered Jerry Madison as a coaching client, he was living in a world with not the most halcyon of circumstances.

As an African-American child raised primarily by a single mother, with a father who was in and out of prison for most of his young life, in a neighborhood with gang members on every corner, and with a metal detector to meet him at school every morning, it would be reasonable to say that the challenges Jerry faced on a day-to-day basis might be insurmountable.

Yet, Jerry had other plans. He was determined to demonstrate that he was bigger than his circumstances. He worked hard in school and sports. He made his faith and spirituality a priority in his life.

He not only made it to college, but he also majored in engineering and emerged a bright, caring, capable young man. As he went out into the world and cultivated a strong and prolific career, he also felt something was missing.

Sure, he was demonstrating that *he* was bigger than his circumstances, but he wanted that demonstration to go beyond *himself.* He wanted to lift his human experience from simply a life well lived to a life elevated through a ministry of inspiring and encouraging challenged youth that they, too, could rise above their circumstances and be successful in this world. His Northstar Intention was to grow a multimedia platform from which all manner of content could blossom in service to his message.

Jerry had moved from what would be a perfectly successful life to one that was illuminated by Soul Purpose. His intention had become clear. Now, it was time to align his actions to his intention and commit to them.

It was in his late 20s that Jerry became a coaching client and one of his first actions, in service of his Northstar Intention, was to craft a Soul Purpose Vision. Without much difficulty, he described an optimal day in the future where his vision of success had been realized. Take notice of how Jerry put an emphasis on his qualitative experience (joy, clarity, ease, love, etc.) versus a list of achievements, knowing that the qualitative experience is ultimately what makes a life worth living:

I wake up with peace, lighthearted and filled with joy. I have full mental clarity. I have my loved one still asleep next to me as I kiss her cheek. I smile when I think of all the good and bad times we've endured but have managed to create a healthy and thriving relationship. I enjoy the fresh air and the rays of the sun on my skin.

I meditate and go through my morning routine effortlessly, bringing me to a spiritual ease that transcends all my worries and cares. My morning workout is amazing. I sweat profusely with some of my closest friends. We laugh, we offer encouragement, and we grow together. I feel healthy and strong. My shower is refreshing and beautiful.

I head to my home office and drink my morning, freshly brewed tea as I write my top three priorities for the day. I do not overthink them. They just flow out of me with ease. There is no rush. I head over to my syndicated radio show and encourage my listeners with a life-changing message of hope. I flow with wisdom and knowledge very peacefully.

I have an excellent brunch with my family and friends. Joy, love, and stories fill the room. I am now on the set of my movie or TV show that I have developed and now star in. The crew works like a well-oiled machine. We push through any rough spots with wisdom and grace. It's so freeing and healing that I don't want to leave, but it's time for my mentorship program. I speak to kids from neighborhoods like the one I grew up in. I inspire, love, and educate with clarity and focus.

I have the amazing opportunity every day to help build an amazing, socially conscious company with one of my best friends. I spread love around the office as I enter it, and the love is poured back into me. I feel blessed to change the world in this way. I end the day with an amazing, fresh, homemade dinner with my family. We are healthy, open, and loving with each other. It's hard for us to stop talking as the day winds down. I peacefully lie in bed with a book and my wife. I slowly drift off to sleep, thankful for my family, my life, and all of its simple blessings.

Creating his Soul Purpose Vision was a powerful first action for Jerry because it, along with his Northstar Intention, helped him discern and prioritize what other actions might be aligned while sending a clear request out into the Universe about what he wanted to manifest.

Next, Jerry created a Soul Purpose Action Plan with initial steps in alignment with his Northstar Intention and Soul Purpose Vision. He committed to this plan and took clear action:

- He developed an affirmation targeted on his vision and incorporated it into his daily meditation and prayer.

- He shifted his traditional work situation to part-time work from home, giving him more space and flexibility to create and lean into new opportunities that were aligned with his intention and vision.

- He started a podcast that began to broadcast stories like his out into the world.

- He took acting classes, knowing that this was a frequent route for people to gain prominence and have a platform from which to make positive impact.

- He also made service a priority, offering support to his friends who were in need so they, too, could ascend out of their circumstances.

One of those friends was a young and hungry director of photography, who had his own vision of rising to be a prominent filmmaker. One day, he asked Jerry if he would act in a concept trailer he was shooting to represent a larger film idea he had. His hope was that the concept and energy of the trailer might become viral on the web and maybe even attract film studios and producers.

As the Universe would have it, that concept trailer was for a modern-day dramatic version of the *The Fresh Prince of Bel-Air*, and Jerry was cast as the main character, Will. It was quite synchronistic that the storyline had so many parallels to Jerry's own journey. This request and opportunity were difficult for Jerry, given his work and other demands. Jerry could have easily passed on the opportunity, but he was present to the creativity of the Universe as it provided this unexpected opportunity in alignment with his own Northstar Intention, Soul Purpose Vision, and his action commitment to be in service to those like him.

The concept trailer was shot and put on the web in the hopes that someone might see it and open a door for Jerry's friend to begin his journey toward being a prominent filmmaker. The concept, the subject, the filming, the acting, and the editing were of such quality that the trailer did go viral.

It was covered by *Rolling Stone, Men's Health, People, Esquire,* and many more media platforms. The entertainment industry was taken by it, and offers of representation and media opportunities began to pour in for Jerry and for the young filmmaker. So much so that Jerry experienced overwhelm with all that was happening in terms of which way to go, which offers to pursue, etc., and brought that into a coaching session. He was encouraged to keep relying on what had gotten him this far—centering on his Soul Purpose Vision, being open to what was coming forward, while not being attached to any preference, not needing to decide until it was time, and acting as a co-creator with his Universe.

What was missing was someone with deep industry experience who could offer Jerry sage and neutral guidance. In the coaching session, Jerry invited the Universe to co-create that with him as well. A day after that session, in a weekly gathering of Kirk's group, "Rumi's Field," Kirk spoke to a participant named Steven about Jerry. Suddenly, Steven lit up and said, "I spent years as an agent and worked with Will Smith on the original *Fresh Prince*. Maybe I can help?" Steven then became Jerry's guide, helping him navigate the complex and often cutthroat world of entertainment. Also out of the woodwork came a prominent acting coach who took on Jerry at a greatly reduced rate and a seasoned screenwriter who asked to write a screenplay with him around his life. Truly, as a result of his commitment to his intention, vision, actions, and feedback from the Universe, Jerry was experiencing Murray's quotation coming to life: "A whole stream of events issues from the decision, raising in one's favor all manner of unforeseen incidents, meetings, and material assistance, which no man could have dreamed would have come his way."

There is still a journey in front of Jerry to fully realize the intended scale of his Soul Purpose Vision, but he is already using his newly found visibility to keep building his platform in order to broadcast hope and inspiration to help youth like him know they can find their way.

This story exemplifies what happens when we center on a Northstar Intention and Soul Purpose Vision for our life, and then bravely align our actions and commit to them with vigor while remaining present and flexible to Divine Guidance. We have witnessed story after story that mirror Jerry's. Each time, we are in awe at how the Universe conspires to provide opportunities to see our Soul Purpose emerge in its full glory.

The question for us now is not whether the Universe will come through, it is whether we will be willing to take actions that take us out of our comfort zone, that push us past our self-imposed limitations, in order for us to be in enthusiastic service to our Soul Purpose.

Soul Purpose Practice

We would like to complete this chapter with activities designed to assist you in developing and engaging with your Soul Purpose Plan. This plan will support you in partnering with your True Self and Spirit in manifesting your Soul's calling and unique contribution in this world.

The foundations of this plan are your Northstar Intention and Soul Purpose Vision, which you will have an opportunity to revisit and refine in the first two activities below. Once these are updated, you can continue on to create your Soul Purpose Action Plan (Activity 3), which includes actions to manifest your Soul Purpose, as well as ways to refine it based upon the feedback you receive from your Universe (Activity 4).

We encourage you to take the time you need with each of these steps. You and your Soul Purpose are worth it!

Refining Your Northstar Intention

As we evolve so, too, does our awareness of our Soul Purpose. It is our hope that in reading this book, you have gained greater clarity regarding your Soul Purpose or around the process for gaining that clarity. In either case, it is useful to revisit your intention to see if there are any refinements that would be helpful prior to creating your Soul Purpose Vision.

We encourage you to set an intention to connect with the love and wisdom of your heart as you answer the following questions.

1. Review your notes from the previous activities you have engaged, including the intention you created for gaining clarity with your Soul Purpose and/or your Northstar Intention.

2. Given your evolved awareness, what is your sense of your True Self calling or Soul Purpose? What is being called through you to be manifested in the world at this time?

3. Now, connect with the wisdom of you heart. You may want to place your hand over your heart to support this connection, or you may want to envision someone you love dearly to call forward your loving. Allow yourself to reside in that space of loving service as you envision your Soul Purpose. From that expanded space, ask your True Self to speak further about your calling. What wisdom, inspiration, or guidance does your True Self have to share?

4. Given all that you have shared and received, take some time now to write or refine your Northstar Intention. The following are prompts to support you, and we encourage you to go with your own language and inner direction:

- My intention is to honor my True Self calling to (include your Soul Purpose here).

- My intention is to be open to new possibilities, inspiration, and guidance in service to my Soul Purpose: (include it here).

- My intention is to easefully connect with and reside in my True Self as I (include your Soul Purpose here).

5. Read your Northstar Intention aloud. What do you experience when you read and hear your intention? How does it line up for you? Be present to the quality of your Northstar Intention. Is it uplifting? If you experience it as "flat" energetically, that signals the opportunity to further refine it, imbuing it with language that inspires and uplifts you.

6. When you feel complete with the process, acknowledge yourself for your willingness and devotion to your Soul Purpose and unique contribution in the world.

Remember to post your Northstar Intention in places that you will see daily so that it remains actively present in your life. Additionally, periodically set aside time, as you have now, to revisit and refine your intention.

Refining Your Soul Purpose Vision

Once you have refined your intention, you are ready to review, update, and add details to your Soul Purpose Vision. You can always refine your vision, so allow yourself to fully and freely respond to the questions below.

To begin, set an intention to reside in the love, wisdom, inspiration, and clarity of your True Self as you answer the following questions:

1. If I were currently living my Soul Purpose, what would I be experiencing?

2. What would I be doing?

3. How would I be feeling?

4. How would I be interacting with others and myself?

5. In what ways would I be serving?

6. What would a typical day in my life look like?

7. Now utilize your responses to the above questions to write a first draft of your Soul Purpose Vision. As you do, be sure to use descriptive language that paints the full, glorious picture. Include details in your vision of what you are seeing, hearing, smelling, feeling, and sensing.

8. Read your Soul Purpose Vision out loud. Is it uplifting? Inspiring? Motivating? (Hint: Remember

your linguistic compass? Now is a good time to take it out and check that your Soul Purpose Vision includes encouraging language and that it is imbued with the love and wisdom of your True Self.)

9. At the bottom or top of your Soul Purpose Vision, include the phrase "This or something better for the highest good of all concerned." This is an important key to conscious Co-creation that we both learned as students at the University of Santa Monica and continue to utilize to this day. In essence, this means that the vision we have created is our best attempt at this time—and it may be a form of our preference—so we are open to an even greater vision more fully aligned with our Soul Purpose, if there is one. And often there is!

10. Once you have refined your Soul Purpose Vision, acknowledge your True Self and Spirit for the blessing of your life and your Soul Purpose.

Developing Your Soul Purpose Action Plan

This final process will support you in clarifying the next steps you would like to commit to as you more fully live your Northstar Intention and Soul Purpose Vision.

To begin, set an intention to reside in your heart and True Self as you complete the following steps.

1. Read your Northstar Intention and Soul Purpose Vision aloud. Take a moment to reside in the inspiration, beauty, and enthusiasm of both.

189

2. Identify at least three *inner* action steps that would support you in living your vision. Inner action steps are ones that connect you more fully with the Higher Consciousness of your True Self and Spirit. For example, engaging in a daily spiritual practice, reading sacred poetry or other uplifting material, taking walks in nature, clearing limiting beliefs, etc. Another wonderful inner action would be to state a daily intention to experience joyful and grace-filled Co-creation with Spirit as you partner together to fulfill your Soul Purpose. (Note: You are not committing to these actions right now, nor are you refining them so that they are doable and trackable at this stage, so give yourself the freedom to explore any that come forward.)

3. Identify at least three *outer* action steps that would support you in your Northstar Intention and Soul Purpose Vision. Outer action steps support you in manifesting your vision of meaningful service in the world. For example, contacting someone who may be of support to your vision, volunteering with a group that is related to your service calling, learning a new skill, etc. (Note: Once again, you are not committing to these actions right now, nor are you refining them so that they are doable and trackable at this stage, so give yourself the freedom to explore any that come forward—even outrageous ones.)

4. Take a moment to connect more fully with your True Self and/or Spirit. Are there any additional action steps or guidance that come forward? Add those to your list of inner or outer actions.

5. Review all your inner and outer action steps. Which of these are you called to move forward with at this time? Star those ones.

6. Refine each starred action so that it meets the five criteria of an effective action step: 1) specific and trackable, 2) doable, 3) floor not ceiling, 4) micro-commitment, and 5) the very next step in front of you.

7. Once you have completed refining all the starred actions steps, ask yourself: Which of these actions am I willing to commit to? Remember, this is a sacred commitment to yourself and your Soul Purpose, so really consider what you are prepared to move forward on. Also, to avoid over-committing to too many actions, consider each action step individually *and* as part of your overall commitment. Trim down if necessary. It is much better to start with fewer commitments that you follow through on than to add a lot of new actions to your already-busy life and breach your word with yourself. The former builds self-trust and integrity, which results in more energy and self-confidence; the latter results in the opposite effect—less energy, self-trust, and confidence.

8. If you are ready to commit to one or more of your action steps, then complete the following sentence: I am willing to commit to: (list each action step) Then, move onto step #10.

9. You may not be willing to commit to any of your actions at this time. That is fine. It is better to be honest

with yourself and *not* make a commitment you will not keep. If you are not ready to make a commitment to any action, you may want to revisit steps #2, #3, and #4 above. It may be that you come up with different inner or outer actions that are more effective. If after revisiting these steps you are still unwilling to commit, this may be a sign that you have bumped up against a mental or emotional block. This is good news as it indicates you have an opportunity for Liberation and growth. We encourage you to revisit the activities to clear mental and emotional blocks in Chapter 3 and 4.

10. Create your Soul Purpose Action Plan in a form that works best for you—to-do list, calendar, etc. As you did with your Soul Purpose Vision, add the following phrase to your Action Plan: "This or something better for the highest good of all concerned."

11. Post your Soul Purpose Action Plan in a place you can view it daily.

12. Acknowledge yourself for your willingness to engage in this process in service to living a life of joy, meaning, and purpose

Receiving Feedback and Evolving Your Soul Purpose Action Plan

In Jerry's real-world story, he followed through on the actions he had committed to in his Soul Purpose Action Plan while staying present to new opportunities and actions. This is a key component of effective Co-creation. Once you take the actions outlined in your Action Plan, respond to the following questions as a way to support your practice of 360° Receptivity. Then, use the feedback you receive to adjust your Action Plan. We encourage you to make the practice below part of your regular review and refinement process:

1. What was your experience in taking the action?

2. What did you learn? What feedback did you receive from the Universe?

3. Are there any adjustments or refinements you want to make?

4. Are there any new action steps that have emerged that you would like to now include in your Soul Purpose Action Plan? (If so, utilize the Developing Your Soul Purpose Action Plan process to clarify, design, and commit to these new action steps.)

5. Update your Soul Purpose Action Plan as needed.

6. Regularly acknowledge yourself and celebrate your wins! Keep in mind, wins come in many forms—the successful completion of the steps you have committed to, the progress you have made, the unexpected gifts you have received, as well as your learning and growth from attempts, mistakes, and course corrections—all of these are intrinsic components of your sacred journey of Soul Purpose.

THE EXQUISITE AND ELEGANT DESIGN

"Our jobs, as Souls of this mortal journey, is to shift the seat of our identity from the lower realm to the upper, from the ego to the Self."

—STEVEN PRESSFIELD

Intention. Liberation. Co-creation.

We have brought these forward as the three essential phases of connecting to and living your Soul Purpose.

1. To connect with our True Self, and from there set an intention that clarifies for us, and for the Creative Intelligence around us, what our Soul Purpose is and how we want to live it every day.

2. Liberate ourselves from old conditioning in the form of judgments, limiting beliefs, and misinterpretations

(mental blocks), as well as the associated emotional blocks that comprise the Story of Limitation, which keeps us shackled to our default life.

3. Commit to action and invite Co-creation with Spirit, and all those around us, to power our actions with providence, serendipity, grace, and flow.

It is important to acknowledge that while we presented these three phases in their most common sequence in this guidebook, in practice, it is not uncommon for these three phases to happen simultaneously, to overlap, or even occur in a different order. That is fine. Now that you are aware of these phases, you can identify them when they are occurring and utilize them in ways that are most supportive for you. You can also watch in gratitude as the Divine presents opportunities for each, following Its own sense of timing in service to your dreams.

Lastly, as much as we would love to take full credit for the brilliance of this three-phase learning design, we cannot. It is a process that has been embedded in the Universe since its very beginning as the essential sequence for the full realization of any being. Whether that being is a human, creature, or plant, it always holds true.

The acorn begins with an inherent intention to become a majestic oak. It liberates itself from that which is comfortable and familiar, its shell and moist earth, to become a sprout that bravely breaks free upward into the unknown of the air. It realizes its final glorious state, a towering and majestic oak, through Co-creation with the Universe spanning all 360 degrees in the form of insects, animals, air, water, and light.

The intention of the caterpillar is to imprison itself and then liberate itself from its chrysalis as moth or butterfly to Co-create indescribable beauty together with the sky that surrounds and lifts it.

The intention of the lion cub to realize its own reign requires that it liberate itself from the pride of its birth to roam the savannah and eventually Co-create a new kingdom with a loving and loyal pride of its own.

Why would you be different from the acorn, caterpillar, or lion?

Why would you be different than other beings in the Universe?

You can be rest assured that this process of Intention, Liberation, and Co-creation, as expressed here in Soul Purpose, has been successfully field-tested since the beginning of time by every actualized being that has ever been or ever will be.

It is not our mechanism; it is the Divine's. All we have done is recognize, acknowledge, and point toward it in service to a growing number of people on this planet seeking to fully be what they were born to be with the intent of elevating the world with their gifts. We are not even the first to have pointed it out. You will see its footprints in the wisdom of the ages—from the ancient inscriptions of the Bhagavad Gita and Genesis, to the recent pages of Joseph Campbell's "Hero's Journey," to the celluloid conversation at the edge of a swamp between a little green majestic "oak" named Yoda and a yet unwilling "acorn" named Luke. All may have used different words on their different surfaces, but the underlying mechanism is universal and uniform:

First the Intention of becoming the fullest and truest version of ourselves.

Then the Liberation from the old skin, stories, and conditioning that no longer align with the glory of what we truly are.

Finally, the Co-creation of each Soul's Purpose through an openhanded invitation to the Divine to manifest it with us. Through us. As us.

And what do we discover when our open hand touches the Divine's and our Soul Purpose is fully realized?

We discover that our Soul Purpose, the purpose of our Soul, is to fully and absolutely experience Itself.

And so, we end as we began. We are here to fully and absolutely experience our true essence of pure Loving and to share this Loving in service to others and our world. We are here to Love and to know ourselves as Love. We are here to know ourselves as the very essence that is the Source of Creation itself.

The miracle, the exquisite and elegant design of this Divine Universe we share, is that the more we seek and move toward this truth, the more we will naturally connect with how our life is to be used for the betterment of our world. And the more we seek to be an agent of purpose, compassion, meaning, and betterment, the more we will move toward the awakening of ourselves as Love.

The miracle, the exquisite and elegant design of this Divine Universe we share, is that when we summon the courage to truly follow our hearts, to follow our joy, to follow what truly brings us alive, then all roads lead home.

All roads are, and lead to, your Soul Purpose.

ACKNOWLEDGMENTS

We would like to acknowledge that the Soul Purpose Method isn't something that *we,* Licia and Kirk, are bringing into the world. It is something that is coming into the world *through* us. And not just through *us,* but through all those who have midwifed it in the form of ideas, inspiration, action, and wisdom, which they have generously shared with us. This abundance of Co-creation and 360° Receptivity informs and enhances our process, as well as the content of our workshops, classes, coaching sessions, and now this very guidebook in your hands. From that awareness, we give our heartfelt thanks…

To Drs. Ron & Mary Hulnick who have masterfully followed their inner calling and Spirit's Guidance to inspire Spiritual Psychology onto the planet, and to the University of Santa Monica staff and community who are our Soul Family.

To Janet Goldstein for sharing her vast expertise and insights in the review of the manuscript.

To Morgan Gist MacDonald and the Paper Raven Books team for their care, dedication, and long hours in turning a manuscript into a book.

To the worldwide participants of the Soul Purpose workshops, and to our students and coaching clients who inspire us with their courage, vulnerability, and willingness to make the ascent.

To Licia's family and friends for the many calls, texts, jokes, and meals that have kept what at times was a daunting process much more lighthearted.

To Kirk's beloved siblings—Peggy, Jim, Holly, and Blair (Tiger)—who still mentor by example every day.

To Cindy Lou Stanbridge-Golin for always answering the call (literally) on Licia's commutes home, and to Marie Beech for her loving wisdom and constant enthusiasm.

To Enso for its generous support of Soul Purpose through its networks and people.

To all the volunteers at our workshops and classes who work tirelessly to ensure every detail is impeccable.

To Lenore Perry, Lyla Morrison, and Lina Yaghi for inspired Soul Purpose branding, graphics, and design.

To Lenore Perry for the exquisite cover design and Jesus Cordero for the elegant and artful interior design of this book.

To Carolyn Freyer-Jones and Stephen McGee for their Soul-Centered coaching and providing the birthplace of Soul Purpose.

To Andras Somogyi, Cedi Ali Rajah, and Erik Borzi for their photo magic.

To all those who provided their Real-World Stories as living proof of the efficacy of these principles and processes.

To Raymond Segrist for his early demonstration of Awakening and his encouragement to ask Spirit for what you want.

To our speakers, Sam Polk, Steve Glenn, Pam Scott, David Angelo, Gina Rudan, Nichol Bradford, Kim Culmone, and Barb Groth, for their inspirational stories.

To Barbara Patterson for providing platforms and audiences to spread the work and wisdom.

To the brave participants at Mattel's "Being Limitless," a Soul Purpose Method workshop.

To Kim Culmone for such powerful exampleship of this work in life and business.

To Ryan Levesque and the ASK team for supporting us in learning more deeply about our audience.

To Michael Ebeling for his encouragement and insights.

To Rumi's Field: Julie, Ray, Steven, Emily, Patti, Andrea, William, James, Bryan, and everyone who has sat in the circle and shared your soul.

To Kirk's Granite Pass Tribe, Church, the Music, and soul brothers, Nage, Jimmy, and Greg, for Divine Connection.

To Spirit for Everything.

ABOUT THE AUTHORS

Kirk Souder, MA, Transformative Coach

Kirk's own journey started when having seemingly "arrived" as President and CEO of a large company, his Soul experienced an emptiness and yearned for more. He then pioneered an ascent to a new life summit that combined inner purpose and meaning with outer impact and abundance. Now as a coach, he sherpas other leaders, entrepreneurs, and creators along that ascent. Those leaders have come from Fortune 500–level companies like Mattel, Google/Alphabet, Amazon, and Uber; innovation-led companies like R/GA and SapientRazorfish; and purpose-led start-ups like Everytable. He has spoken and led workshops on leadership transformation and positive impact in places like Hong Kong, Copenhagen, Los Angeles, and New York.

Kirk has a master's degree in Spiritual Psychology, has professional coaching training in technologies such as Three Principles and Success Intelligence, and is a certified graduate of the University of Santa Monica's Soul-Centered Professional Coaching Program. He volunteers multiple times a year inside a women's maximum security prison in a mindset workshop called Freedom to Choose. As a survivor of a five-year journey with stage-four sarcoma, he also coaches people with cancer on how to convert that experience into their own enlightenment and freedom. Kirk lives in Topanga, California with his soulmate, Patricia, and their two sons, McKinley and Kevin.

Licia Rester, LCMFT, Transformative Coach

Licia's inner calling to serve and inspire others has been a guiding light throughout her career. As a facilitator, faculty member, and trainer, Licia has had the privilege of supporting thousands of students, professionals, and online learners in transforming their consciousness and their lives. Licia's love for transformational and innovative education extends to her work as well, as a professional writer and instructional designer. For close to 30 years, she has written, designed, and produced numerous educational video series, in-person classes and programs, and award-winning interactive experiences, including business workshops, university courseware, online classrooms, psychology software, and children's e-learning products. Her clients have included Microsoft, American Express, NBC, Hanna-Barbera Productions, Philips, Interactive Media, Honda, Volvo, Amgen, University of Southern California, and University of Santa Monica.

Licia holds a master's degree in Counseling Psychology from the University of Santa Monica, as well as certifications in Soul-Centered Leadership; Consciousness, Health & Healing; and Soul-Centered Professional Coaching. She is also a Licensed Clinical Marriage and Family Therapist and transformative coach. In her private practice, she works with individuals and groups in clarifying, creating, and living an inspired and inspiring life. Licia lives in Southern California with her husband and soul partner, David, and they enjoy dancing, listening to music, laughing with family and friends, and serving the Beloved.

Kirk, Licia, and Soul Purpose

Kirk and Licia met in 2010, when they were joined in initiatives to bring the Principles and Practices of Spiritual Psychology into the world. Later, in answering a calling to meet the growing number of leaders seeking purpose, Kirk sought to scale his work to the level of conferences and workshops and reached out to Licia for her expertise in curriculum and program design. From that, the Soul Purpose Method was born, as well as a prolific, authentic relationship, divinely united in serving individuals in awakening to their True Selves, Soul Purpose, and the limitless potential to positively impact the world.

CPSIA information can be obtained
at www.ICGtesting.com
Printed in the USA
BVHW040826240919
559158BV00010B/8/P